Spies Among Us

SPIES
THE TRUTH ABOUT
AMONG
MODERN ESPIONAGE
US

BY HERMA SILVERSTEIN

FRANKLIN WATTS

New York   London   Toronto   Sydney   1988

ST. PHILIP'S COLLEGE LIBRARY

Photographs courtesy of:
AP/Wide World Photos: pp. 14, 26, 37, 45, 47, 52,
69, 77, 94, 99, 103, 112, 126;
UPI/Bettmann Newsphotos: pp. 18, 55, 65, 87, 91, 121.

Book design by Jackie Schuman

Library of Congress Cataloging-in-Publication Data

Silverstein, Herma.
Spies among us : the truth about modern espionage / by Herma
Silverstein.
p.   cm.
Bibliography: p.
Includes index.
Summary: Examines the world of modern espionage, discussing the functions of intelligence agencies around the world, how and why they gather information, and examples of spy operations and famous cases.
ISBN 0-531-10600-4
1. Intelligence service—Juvenile literature. 2. Espionage—
Juvenile literature. 3. Spies—Juvenile literature.
[1. Intelligence service. 2. Espionage. 3. Spies.] I. Title.
JF1525.I6S55   1988
327.1'2—dc19   88-5546   CIP   AC

Copyright © 1988 by Herma Silverstein
All rights reserved
Printed in the United States of America
5 4 3 2 1

*To Caroline Arnold
with love and thanks
for planting a bug in my ear*

Contents

1
James Bond Unmasked: The Truth about Modern Espionage
11

2
The Making of an American Spy: What the CIA Is All About
25

3
The Making of a Russian Spy: What the KGB Is All About
36

4
The Atom Spies: Espionage in the 1950s
44

5
More Atom Spies: The Aftermath of the Rosenberg Trial
53

6
Spies by Land or by Sea: Espionage Exposures in the 1960s
60

7
Going Over to the Other Side: Spies Who Defect
72

8
In from the Cold: Swapping Captured Spies
84

9
Of Spies and Satellites: Espionage in the 1970s
98

10
Bugs, Subs, and Lasers: Modern Spy Gadgets
108

11
A Family Affair: The John Walker Spy Ring
118

Notes 131
Glossary of Spy Terms 135
Further Reading 139
Index 141

Spies Among Us

1
James Bond Unmasked: The Truth about Modern Espionage

Yes, there really was a James Bond—according to many British intelligence agents, that is. Author Ian Fleming allegedly based his character James Bond on a real man named James Boone, an administrative inspector in the British Foreign Office. While Boone's actual job involved examining supplies stored at British diplomatic missions in the Middle East and Africa, he pretended to his girlfriends that his dull inspector's job was a cover for his *real* job, which he said involved dangerous spy operations.

James Boone did in fact become famous, but his notoriety was gained by accident. One night, while working at a British mission in Teheran, Iran, a drunk man started molesting Boone's girlfriend. Boone killed the man with a single karate chop. It was later discovered that the drunk was a heroin smuggler wanted in five countries. From then on, Boone supposedly lived in a fantasy world, convinced that his invented, life-threatening exploits were real.

Spying is as old as history. The Bible speaks of God telling Moses to send twelve agents to "spy out the land of Canaan," (Numbers 13) and Delilah was a spy for the Philistines. In 400 B.C., the Chinese commentator, Sun-tzu, wrote *The Art of War*, in which he discussed five kinds of intelligence agents. Around 218 B.C., the Carthaginian general, Hannibal, sent a spy who pretended to join Hannibal's Roman enemies into a walled city in Sicily. At night, the spy built a campfire and used a blanket to send smoke signals to Hannibal.

In the fifteenth century, the Italian city-states used foreign

SPIES AMONG US

ambassadors as spies and developed secret codes to communicate information. In the sixteenth century, Sir Francis Walsingham, secretary of state to Queen Elizabeth I of England, developed a network of intelligence agents in foreign lands that became the forerunner of today's intelligence organizations.

The first modern intelligence agency was formed by Britain in 1910. Germany followed in 1913, and Russia in 1917. While the American Revolution had such spies for and against the colonies as Nathan Hale and Benedict Arnold, it was not until 1947 that the United States established an official, permanent intelligence agency, named the Central Intelligence Agency (CIA).

One of the best-known spies of all time was Mata Hari, a Dutch woman who became an Indian dancer in Paris where, during World War I, she spied on France for Germany. Mata Hari became the mistress of the French war minister, from whom she extracted top secret information that she passed on to the Germans. She was caught by the French and executed by a firing squad in 1917.

One of the most brilliant spies of World War II was Communist Richard Sorge, who posed as a Nazi foreign correspondent in Tokyo. Sorge tipped off Russian dictator Joseph Stalin to Hitler's invasion of Russia and the Japanese attack on Pearl Harbor. Sorge's information was not believed by Stalin and he was eventually caught and executed in Tokyo.

Today, spying is one of the world's biggest industries. The CIA spends approximately 1.5 billion dollars a year on intelligence gathering and operations, and employs around 150,000 people. Russia's KGB is estimated to spend close to 1.7 billion dollars and to employ approximately 1 million people, while Britain's annual intelligence budget is approximately 500 million dollars, with 25,000 employees. This adds up to a total figure worldwide of at least 1,175,000 people involved in some capacity with spying.

Why are so many people involved in spying? Part of the answer may lie in novels and films about espionage that foster the image of the spy as romantic and daring, and a career in espionage as glamorous and exciting. Some people believe that

James Bond Unmasked: The Truth about Modern Espionage

being a spy is equal to being a screen star. Instead of thousands of adoring fans, the spy believes he or she will automatically be fawned over by members of the opposite sex. For women who are not outwardly attractive, or men who are not like James Bond, becoming a spy is a way of making romantic and exciting things happen to them that probably would not occur if they were employed in an ordinary occupation.

One such man was Richard Miller, the first FBI agent ever to be charged with espionage. Miller was the complete opposite of macho. He weighed over 250 pounds. At the time of his arrest in 1985, he was on suspension from the FBI for being overweight and for being a bumbling agent, always behind in his work and frequently losing his badge. When a beautiful Russian immigrant, Svetlana Ogorodnikova, seemingly fell in love with him, Miller was able to play out his James Bond fantasies, and in exchange for sexual favors agreed to give her top-secret FBI documents. When he was arrested, Miller claimed he gave Svetlana the documents in order to become the first FBI agent to infiltrate the KGB. He called his plan a "James Bond fantasy."[1] He was sentenced to two life prison terms, plus fifty years.

Besides the belief that all spies look and act like male or female James Bonds, another myth about intelligence agents derived from spy novels and films is the belief that intelligence officers wear disguises to penetrate "enemy" territory. In fact, only a small percentage of intelligence officers carry concealed weapons, hidden cameras, coded messages on microdots sewn into the lining of their clothes, or other spy gadgets that, if discovered, would expose these agents as spies. One of the intelligence officer's main objectives is to avoid being identified as an intelligence officer.

Real spies are human beings, with human emotions. Therefore, it cannot be assumed that spies are flawless, that after completing an intelligence agency's required courses in spying, espionage agents will have been drilled hard enough to wipe out all their character weaknesses and human emotions. People's feelings cannot be completely eliminated simply by tough intelligence training.

Svetlana Ogorodnikova presents a glamorous image of a spy. In 1985 she admitted to conspiracy to commit espionage and was sentenced to eighteen years in prison.

Many times, in fact, such human emotions as greed, love, and anger have caused spies to give themselves away. One such person was Reino Hayhanen, Russian spy Rudolf Abel's associate, who was an alcoholic. His dependency upon alcohol led him to break down and confess under questioning by Western intelligence agents.

Thus, in spite of newspaper stories about the true lives of intelligence agents—most of them are ordinary people, earning too little to afford expensive houses, cars, and other luxuries—

James Bond Unmasked: The Truth about Modern Espionage

the "James Bond Myth" of espionage careers being romantic and exciting continues, luring countless people into working for intelligence agencies. The myth also persists because of misconceptions about what spies and intelligence organizations do. Espionage means spying. Intelligence means information, often secret, that is gathered and analyzed about another country's military capabilities, scientific achievements, or other affairs of state. The analyzed information is used to compare military strengths or to determine foreign policy.

To obtain this information, every country has its own intelligence organizations, such as the United States' CIA, the Soviet Union's KGB and GRU, France's Service de Documentation Exterieure et de Contre-Espionage (SDECE), and Israel's Mossad. Great Britain's two main intelligence agencies are the Security Service, called MI5, which handles domestic intelligence operations, and the Secret Intelligence Service (SIS), called MI6, which handles foreign intelligence operations. And while there is no such British Director of MI6 as James Bond's "M," which stands for the fictional Admiral Sir Miles Messervy, there was a "C," named after the first head of MI6, Sir Mansfield Cumming.

Germany's intelligence organization was originally composed of former Nazis. In 1945, German General Reinhard Gehlen, commander of a German army intelligence section, took his men and files, surrendered to the Americans, and offered to use his espionage network in Soviet territory to work for America's military intelligence organization, the Office of Strategic Services (OSS). Thus was created the Gehlen Organization, headquartered in Frankfurt, West Germany, where it pursued espionage operations against the Communists even while the Soviet Union was still a U.S. ally.

After the war, the OSS and Great Britain's SIS continued to recruit former Gestapo officers for the Gehlen Organization, as these men could help identify other Nazis in hiding. One example was former Nazi Klaus Barbie, called the "Butcher of Lyon" for ordering thousands of Jews to their deaths at German concentration camps. The British and American governments rewarded Barbie for his spying by giving him a new identity and helping him "disappear." Barbie lived in freedom and anonymity for forty years before he was caught, tried, and found guilty for crimes against humanity in 1987. General Gehlen retired in 1968, and his organization was renamed the German Federal Intelligence Service.

There are many ways for intelligence agencies to obtain information—from human espionage, to satellites, to alternate means such as newspapers, scientific or military journals, official public records, and reports from foreign correspondents, diplomats, and military attachés.

With so many alternate means available to intelligence officers, it would seem that there is little left for spies to do. But the fact is that espionage organizations often have more operations than they have spies to carry them out. Besides gathering intelligence, a second function of intelligence agencies is counterintelligence. This involves getting information about foreign espionage operations and preventing foreign spies from penetrating the agency and stealing secret information.

The third job of intelligence agencies is carrying out covert, or secret, political operations, which involve manipulating the internal affairs of other nations. While this book is concerned mainly with espionage and counterespionage, some examples of covert operations must be mentioned, as these acts have affected the structure and power of intelligence agencies over the years.

The CIA's covert operations, for example, usually involve trying to suppress a Communist regime in a third world country, including the ouster or assassination of the country's leader. The CIA is believed to have participated in the overthrow of Communist governments in Iran in 1953 and Guatemala in 1954; in the 1961 assassinations of General Rafael Trujillo, dictator of the Dominican Republic, and Patrice Lumumba, prime minister of Zaire, once the Congo; and in the 1963 assassination of South Vietnam's President Ngo Dinh Diem. Moreover, during the Vietnam war, to help overthrow the North Vietnamese government, the CIA ran airline companies at a profit of 50 million dollars and organized a private army in Laos. The Agency also helped promote the 1973 coup that resulted in the overthrow and death of Chile's Marxist president Salvador Allende.

James Bond Unmasked: The Truth about Modern Espionage

In the United States, the CIA was linked to the 1972 Republican-sponsored break-in and theft of files of the Democratic national headquarters in the Washington hotel complex called the Watergate—thus the name "Watergate Scandal." Two of those arrested, James McCord and E. Howard Hunt, were CIA employees.

In 1961, the CIA trained and equipped Cuban exiles for an invasion of Cuba at the Bay of Pigs, in an attempt to overthrow the Marxist government of Cuban Premier Fidel Castro. It is now known that the CIA purposely withheld information from President John Kennedy that the chances of a successful invasion were slim. Instead, then CIA Director Allen Dulles convinced Kennedy that Cuban anti-Communist rebels would back up American troops once they landed at the Bay of Pigs. This did not happen, and the invasion was a disaster, ending in Dulles being replaced by John McCone, who had been chairman of the Atomic Energy Commission.

Critics blamed the failure on the CIA's trying both to run the covert operation and to analyze its chances for success, since there is a natural inclination to predict the success of an operation one is in charge of. President Kennedy was so angry at the CIA's duplicity that he threatened to "splinter the CIA into a thousand pieces and scatter it to the winds."[2]

In 1986, the CIA again withheld vital information from an American president to promote illegal, covert activities. In 1984, Congress had passed a law banning direct military assistance to rebel troops in Nicaragua, called *contras*, who were fighting Nicaragua's Communist Sandinista government. In November 1986, although President Reagan had publicly stated that his administration would not deal with terrorists, it was discovered that members of the CIA and the National Security Council (NSC) had nevertheless been secretly selling arms to Iran in the hope of obtaining the release of American hostages held by Shi'ite Muslim terrorists in Lebanon. In addition, these American officials were using some of the profits from these sales to buy weapons and supplies for the contras, which was against the 1984 law. These supplies were delivered with the aid of CIA covert operations officers in Honduras and Costa Rica.

Lieutenant Colonel Oliver North became a media hero in 1987 during his week of televised testimony in the Iran-Contra arms hearings.

The instigators of the Iran scheme were the then director of the CIA, William Casey, former National Security Council adviser Admiral John Poindexter, and his aide, Lieutenant Colonel Oliver North. In spite of a federal law requiring a signed presidential "finding," or approval, for every CIA covert operation, and notification of Congress "in a timely fashion," neither Congress nor, allegedly, President Reagan were informed of the operation.[3]

In fact, Claire George, the CIA's chief of secret operations, told congressional investigating committees that the CIA had no knowledge of the weapons airlifts to the contras. Alan D. Fiers, chief of CIA operations in Central America, later admitted he also lied to Congress about his allowing his officers to assist the contras with weapons. Moreover, CIA Director Casey lied to President Reagan by telling him that Iran was cutting back on terrorism, and Soviet influence in Iran was growing, in order to convince Reagan that the United States should provide weapons to Iran as a countermeasure. It was also discovered that, without congressional approval, the CIA was negotiating with Iran for the release of Iranian terrorists imprisoned in Kuwait in exchange for the release of American hostages.

If the contra affair had not become public, Admiral Poindexter and William Casey had planned to establish a secret, independent government unit, funded by private citizens, to carry out covert operations around the world. North described this unit as an "off-the-shelf, self-sustaining entity known as Project Democracy."[4]

As in the CIA's failed Bay of Pigs invasion, the Agency was trying to provide objective intelligence at the same time that it was attempting to make foreign policy based upon that intelligence. As Secretary of State George Shultz said: "One lesson from the scandal is separating the gathering and analyzing of intelligence from . . . developing and carrying out of policy . . . it is too tempting to have your analysis . . . favor the policy that you're advocating."[5]

As a result of what came to be known as the "Iran Contra Scandal," there is a proposal to ban the CIA from carrying out all paramilitary operations. In addition, the scandal again raised questions about how much power and secrecy intelligence agencies should have. As Senator George J. Mitchell (Democrat-Maine), a member of the congressional committee investigating the scandal, said to Colonel Oliver North: "People have a right to know what the government is doing. You have talked here . . . of the need for a democratic outcome in Nicaragua. Many patriotic Americans are concerned that in the pursuit of democracy abroad, we do not compromise it in any way at home."[6]

If real intelligence agents' lives bear little resemblance to James Bond's, why do some people believe spies lead a Bond type of life? While many of the myths about the CIA's spy operations are created by Communist countries to use as propaganda against the United States, most misconceptions about Western intelligence operations persist because people like to believe in heroes. The continued popularity of the fictional hero Superman is one example of this desire. Further, most people lead routine lives that may seem dull compared to that of the hero in a spy novel. Reading or seeing a film about a person who leads an excitement-packed life is a way of experiencing the thrills many people wish would occur in their own lives.

But, contrary to spy novels and films, when spies are caught, their exposure is rarely the result of trickery by an "enemy" espionage agent. Usually a spy is exposed by defectors from the spy's own intelligence agency, who inform on him or her. Other times spies are caught because they are noticeably living beyond the salaries they make at their regular jobs, which arouses suspicions about where the extra money is coming from. And, other times the culprit is the spy's carelessness, or the spy's neighbor or friend who unknowingly gives him or her away.

For example, one Soviet spy was exposed when he sent a suit to the cleaners and forgot to remove a stolen U.S. Navy intelligence document from the pants pocket. The cleaner discovered the document and turned it over to authorities. In another instance, a well-meaning landlady thought she would do one of her boarders a favor by taking a pair of his shoes to be repaired because they were worn through on the soles. When the cobbler removed the old heels, he found them to be hollow compartments containing strips of paper with writing on them.

Occasionally the spy's exposure is due to a gadget that fails to work as planned. Among such examples are a suitcase with a false bottom that falls apart under rough handling by a customs inspector; an invisible writing pen that fails to work; or a document carried by the spy that is discovered by customs inspectors to be forged. In other instances, spies get caught by sheer chance, such as being in an airplane crash or an automobile accident.

In 1941, a Nazi spy working in America was struck and killed by a taxi. His accomplice ran from the scene. A notebook found on the deceased's body revealed he was a German masquerading as a Spaniard. A short time later, a postal censorship inspector in Bermuda found a reference to the accident in some suspicious looking correspondence that was regularly being sent from the United States to Spain. The inspector informed the FBI, whose investigation exposed the Nazi spy ring of Kurt F. Ludwig. Ludwig was the accomplice who had left the scene of the accident, and who was mailing secret information to Spain about the United States.

The most frequent espionage mishaps occur when communication attempts between spies fail. Messages intended for intelligence agents are often left in secret places, called "drops." There are two kinds of drops: "dead drops," places where messages are left by one agent to be picked up later by another agent; and "live drops," couriers who pass messages back and forth between agents.

Occasionally what seems like a safe dead drop when an agent leaves a message becomes unsafe before the other agent can get there to pick it up. In one case an agent left a message in a public restroom stall. Before the second agent arrived to retrieve the message, the cleaning staff had turned that stall into a supply closet and put a lock on the door. At other times a courier's train or plane is late, and the courier arrives too late to deliver a message to an agent who has been instructed to wait only a certain amount of time. Mishaps of this nature can result in the espionage mission being "blown," or uncovered.

In contrast to the many myths about spies, there are some spy facts that are true to life. Coded messages, numbers used for spies' names, such as James Bond's "007," and drops used to deposit messages are some examples. Rudolf Abel's assistant, Reino Hayhanen, let Abel know he had arrived in the United States from the Soviet Union by sticking a thumbtack into a sign in front of Fort Tryon Park in upper Manhattan. In addition, Abel and Hayhanen chose dramatic places for drops, such as the underside of a telephone booth in a Manhattan bar, a magnetized container stuck to a seldom used gate in Brooklyn's Prospect Park, and cracks in concrete staircases.

Rudolf Abel used the code name "Mark," and Hayhanen the name "Vic." The risk in such cases is the chance encounter with someone who knows the agent by his true name, and blurts it out upon seeing the agent. The American couple who were members of Russian spy Gordon Lonsdale's spy ring called themselves the Krogers. They were recognized by a retired football coach when *Life* magazine published an article about the spy ring, along with photographs of everyone arrested in the case. The coach phoned the FBI saying he recognized the man Kroger as the same boy who had tried out for his high school football team thirty-five years earlier. But the spy's name was not Kroger.

If romance and glamour motivate people to become spies for their countries, what motivates people who betray their countries? In the past, many spies claimed ideological reasons. In the 1930s, there was a movement toward sympathy for the poor and unemployed masses, and a hatred of capitalism. Many people turned to the socialist ideals of Communism, which they believed would benefit mankind. Thus, the Soviets recruited England's most notorious spies—Kim Philby, Guy Burgess, Donald Maclean, and Anthony Blunt—to become spies within British intelligence organizations. The so-called atom bomb spies of the 1950s such as Klaus Fuchs said they gave the Russians information about America's scientific developments for humanitarian purposes, believing such knowledge should be shared with the world.

Today enough is known about the true meaning of Communism that no one can realistically claim to be spying for the Communists in order to save the world. Spies of the 1980s, such as the John Walker family, who sold U.S. Navy secrets to the Soviets, were more motivated by the presumed glamour, thrills, and the money to be made from espionage. Most likely, the spies of the 1930s through 1950s also had materialistic motives behind their professed ideology, imagining that they alone would become the heroes or heroines who saved the world by showing capitalists the "evil" of their former ways. Even American Jonathan J. Pollard, who claimed he stole U.S. data about terrorists and sold it to Israel out of a Zionist motivation to help the Jewish state, eventually found himself spying for the romantic self-image he got from his espionage.

James Bond Unmasked: The Truth about Modern Espionage

Often, out of a desperate need for money, people decide that they will betray their country only once, and then stop. However, once into the spy game, they continue because they fear getting caught, or because they are being blackmailed by spies of the country to which they give information, or because they get embroiled in the many lies that must be told in order to cover up their spying. These cover-ups must then be covered up. As more people become involved, such as accomplices and witnesses, the cycle seems never to end.

One example is the elaborate cover-up employed by participants in the Iran contra scandal, which included shredding of classified documents and writing false reports. These cover-ups led to the involvement of secretaries and other low-level employees of the CIA and the National Security Council.

Concerning today's spies' motives of thrills, romance, and greed, former CIA analyst George Carver says, "We've lost the sense . . . that there are things you simply don't do. . . . One of them is that you don't betray your country."[7]

Adding to the romantic or monetary lure of spying is the mysterious aura of working for organizations that are cloaked in secrecy. While intelligence officials insist that secrecy is the key to protecting national security, believing that secret knowledge is secret power, many other people view such strict secrecy as a means of allowing intelligence agencies to wield an overabundance of power. For example, from 1967 until 1973, the CIA carried out Operation CHAOS, in which the Agency collected information about dissident Americans who were protesting the Vietnam War.

During this time the CIA also opened mail between the United States and the Soviet Union, and, without warrants, used wiretaps to eavesdrop on Americans' telephone conversations, and broke into their homes and offices. The Agency claimed it was only spying on people who might be a threat to national security, but under questioning by a congressional committee, CIA officers admitted that they frequently listened in on telephone calls simply to eavesdrop.

Critics of the power of the intelligence services cite their underworld sections. In the CIA, this branch is called the Office of Special Operations, or more commonly, the "Department of Dirty Tricks." Dirty tricks include robbery, maiming, torture, and murder—either in cold blood, or by an "accident." Many enemy spies have been killed "accidentally" by being run over by a car, thrown off a speeding train, or pushed over a ship's railing. Another dirty trick is the administration of drugs to sedate enemy agents in order to kidnap them or search their homes and offices for intelligence secrets. In the early 1970s, for example, the CIA was found to have experimented with drugs such as LSD on unwitting victims.

Real spies, then, are usually not macho superheroes or glamorous, cunning heroines found in novels and films. Their time is filled more with gathering painstaking details than with daring adventure. Their hours are long, their jobs insecure, their salaries insufficient compared to the risks taken, and, for the most part, the only excitement in their lives occurs when they are caught. As far as heroes are concerned, only spies who get caught make headlines.

As General Walter Bedell Smith, the second director of the CIA, said: "A CIA agent cannot hope to be a hero. All he can win is a notation on a secret record: 'Well done.' "[8]

Even so, spying continues. The inherent glamour associated with being a spy for or against one's country has kept the lure of becoming a spy alive for centuries. And, unless some catastrophic event occurs that erases this enticement of romantic, dangerous adventure, there will continue to be spies and espionage.

2
The Making of an American Spy: What the CIA Is All About

Sometime in 1984, twenty-two year-old Clayton Lonetree, a Marine guard at the U.S. Embassy in Moscow, began having an affair with Violetta Sanni, a Russian translator for the embassy. In December 1986, Lonetree went to his superiors at the American Embassy in Vienna to which he had been transferred, and told them a story that exploded into the first espionage scandal to hit the U.S. Marine Corps since its creation in 1775. For Violetta Sanni had purposely become sexually involved with Clayton Lonetree to get him to spy for the Soviet Union. Thus, the affair came to be known as the "Marine Sex for Secrets Case." In return for his spying, Lonetree received $3,500 from a KGB agent, code named "Uncle Sasha."

Clayton J. Lonetree was convicted for providing the Soviet Union with the identities of CIA agents in Moscow, and the floor plans to the U.S. embassies in Moscow and Vienna. He was given a thirty-year prison sentence. At his trial, Lonetree claimed that he had given nothing of value to the Soviets and had dealt with the KGB because after reading many spy novels he fantasized about becoming a double agent and exposing the KGB.

To assess the damage, the remaining Marine guards at U.S. consulates and embassies in the Soviet Union were recalled to the United States for questioning. The scandal was partly blamed on an inadequate security system at the Moscow embassy. Officials had been warned as early as 1983 that the security system there was so slipshod that the KGB could easily penetrate the building. Yet nothing was done to remedy the situation. In 1985,

Marine Corps Sergeant Clayton Lonetree was one of the key figures in connection with the 1987 discovery of bugging at the American embassy in Moscow.

KGB listening devices were discovered inside embassy typewriters, which, via an antenna hidden in the chimney, were transmitting typed messages to the Soviets in Washington.

On April 11, 1987, a grave result from the spy scandal was revealed—the KGB had executed at least six Russian citizens

The Making of an American Spy: What the CIA Is All About

working secretly for U.S. intelligence agencies. The deaths put an end to some of the United States' most valuable intelligence operations inside Soviet territory. The Russians' names were assumed to have been given to the KGB by Clayton Lonetree. Some U.S. officials believe that if Lonetree had not confessed, the case might never have been exposed. Lonetree admitted his involvement with the KGB only after he mistakenly thought one of his meetings with Soviet agents in Vienna had been bugged by the CIA, and thus believed the CIA had found him out. Actually, the bugging was instigated by the KGB to check whether any U.S. intelligence agents were on their trail.

The exposure of the "Sex for Secrets" spy scandal spurred U.S. intelligence services to use more extensive screening of applicants for top security positions, tighter counterintelligence measures to spot employees vulnerable to Soviet recruitment, and regular polygraph tests to catch employees who might have been recruited by the KGB.

As more aggressive counterintelligence measures were begun, giving the CIA greater power to run spy operations, the CIA has come full circle from its beginnings, when Americans' mistrust of spying in general stalled the CIA's creation, and then limited the Agency's power once it was finally created.

Until 1947, espionage in the United States was mostly a wartime activity, in which special military intelligence units were created for each branch of the armed services to get military secrets from the enemy. When a war ended, these units were disbanded. During the American Revolution, most espionage activities were performed by private citizens who volunteered to collect military information about the British. One of the first American double agents (a person claiming to work for one government, but in reality working for an enemy government) was Dr. Edward Bancroft. Posing as Benjamin Franklin's secretary in France, while Franklin attempted to enlist French aid for the colonists, Bancroft gave information to the British about Franklin's negotiations.

Bancroft also was one of the first spies known to use a "drop" for leaving secret messages. He wrote his messages in invisible ink between the lines of fake love letters, which he left in the hollowed out root of a tree in the Tuileries Gardens in Paris. Later, General George Washington organized a secret intelligence bureau headed by Robert Townsend and Major Benjamin Tallmadge. Their efforts were responsible for catching British spy Benedict Arnold.

The idea of an intelligence service separate from the military was not thought about until 1861, when conspirators from Baltimore, Maryland, were discovered plotting to assassinate President Abraham Lincoln on the way to his inauguration. Allan Pinkerton, a private detective who later created the Pinkerton Detective Agency, was hired to protect the President.

After the Union Army's defeat at Antietam during the Civil War, a precursor of today's secret service, named the National Detective Police, was created. The organization was headed by Lafayette Baker, a Union spy who posed as a traveling photographer of Confederate soldiers while he gathered intelligence about the South's war strategy. Baker's fame, however, was for his failure to prevent Lincoln's assassination. To this day there is a mystery about where Baker and his Detective Police were the night of April 14, 1865, when Lincoln was assassinated as he watched a play at Ford's Theater.

After the Civil War, the United States created its first peacetime military intelligence organizations, the army's Military Information Division (M.I.D.), and the navy's Office of Secret Intelligence (OSI). It was also at this time that America's first military and naval attachés were sent to U.S. embassies abroad to conduct intelligence operations. In 1903, the Army General Staff was created as a permanent army intelligence division, and the M.I.D. was incorporated into it as a "Second Division." Hence the name G-2, which is still used today to mean Army Intelligence.

By the end of World War I, U.S. military intelligence branches included G-2, the Office of Naval Intelligence (O.N.I.), and a counterespionage organization called the Corps of Intelligence Police. Yet Americans rated espionage so low an occupation that no further efforts were made to create a nonmilitary centralized intelligence agency. In fact, there was not even a U.S. law concerning espionage against the United States until the passage of the Espionage Act of 1917. America's backwardness in its intelligence development prompted Secretary of State Dean Acheson to say in 1945 that "The State Department's technique of gathering information differs only by reason of the typewriter and telegraph from the techniques which John Quincy Adams was using in St. Petersburg. . . ."[1]

Between the two World Wars, the only centralized intelligence activity in America was the State Department's "Black Chamber," a decoding unit. Because of antiespionage sentiment, Henry L. Stimson, secretary of state under President Herbert Hoover, eventually closed the Black Chamber, saying, "Gentlemen do not read other gentlemen's mail."[2] Nevertheless, a small group of American cryptographers (code breakers) continued to perfect their craft and thereby provided the United States with one of its most vital weapons when America entered World War II—the skills necessary to break the Japanese naval codes.

In 1955, a congressional committee investigating the CIA, called the Hoover Commission Task Force, issued a report, part of which said: "The Central Intelligence Agency may well attribute its existence to the surprise attack on Pearl Harbor and to the postwar investigations into the part intelligence or lack of intelligence played in the failure of our military to receive adequate and prompt warning of the impending Japanese attack."[3]

The surprise Japanese attack on Pearl Harbor forced government officials to recognize the need for a centralized secret intelligence agency, independent of military intelligence organizations. Individual warnings about the attack had gone unheeded because there was no centralized agency to put these warnings together, and which most likely would have come to the conclusion that a Japanese attack was imminent. These warnings included the facts that the U.S. ambassador in Tokyo had heard rumors of an attack; the FBI knew that a Japanese agent in Honolulu was keeping track of every U.S. ship; and U.S. cryptographers, who had cracked the Japanese code, knew that two Japanese ambassadors in Washington were about to break off negotiations with the United States.

Thus, on December 7, 1941, the Japanese successfully put the bulk of the U.S. fleet out of action. After Pearl Harbor, President Franklin Roosevelt asked Colonel William J. Donovan (known as "Wild Bill" Donovan), a World War I U.S. Army Medal of Honor recipient, who had become a distinguished attorney, to establish a centralized intelligence agency. By June 1942, the Office of Strategic Services (OSS) was founded, with Donovan as its chief. The job of the OSS was to "collect and analyze strategic information and to plan and operate special services."[4]

The term "special services" was a cover-up phrase for all secret intelligence operations, which then included planning the invasion of North Africa and parachuting behind enemy lines to help anti-Nazi underground groups. After the War, the OSS was responsible for capturing war criminals and interrogating German counterintelligence officers to learn which American spies the Germans had turned into double agents. In 1944, Donovan proposed to President Roosevelt that a permanent intelligence agency be created. In April 1945, a week before Roosevelt died, he asked Donovan to bring together OSS chiefs to get their opinions about such an agency.

Yet after Roosevelt's death, President Harry Truman disbanded the OSS, transferring its functions to the State Department and the Department of War, believing a "cloak and dagger" agency in peacetime was nonessential. However, the need for some kind of intelligence organization was thought necessary, and Truman established the Central Intelligence Group (CIG) in January 1946, which lasted twenty months, and became the direct predecessor to the CIA.

Between 1945 and 1950, Stalin placed Communist governments in Poland, Rumania, Bulgaria, Hungary, and Czechoslovakia; threatened to overthrow Iran; instigated civil war in Greece; and established the Berlin blockade. American intelligence officers stressed to President Truman that it was vital to U.S. national security to learn all they could about Soviet plans to foster Communism worldwide. In an address to Congress on March 12, 1947, Truman recommended that a central intelligence agency

The Making of an American Spy: What the CIA Is All About

be created as a permanent agency of the government. Congress approved by passing the National Security Act of 1947.

This act replaced the CIG with the Central Intelligence Agency (CIA); united all military services under a Defense Department headed by a secretary of Defense; created the National Security Council (NSC), composed of the President, vice president, the directors of the CIA and the Office of Defense Mobilization, and the secretaries of State and Defense. The CIA would be run by a director and a deputy director, both appointed by the President and subject to Senate confirmation. The CIA would act only on directives given it by the President and the National Security Council, and would be responsible to the House and Senate Armed Forces and Appropriations committees.

Although the CIA is mainly a fact-finding agency that evaluates and analyzes information about other countries, misinterpretation of the word intelligence to mean espionage has led many people to believe the CIA is strictly a spying organization. In reality, only one branch of the CIA, the Office of Special Operations (OSO), handles spying, being responsible for espionage, counterespionage, and covert political operations. Moreover, to make sure the CIA never became a secret police organization, Congress denied the CIA the power to arrest suspects, to subpoena witnesses, or to use any other law enforcement powers. In contrast, U.S. military intelligence agencies possess all the law enforcement powers of any police force.

The CIA categorizes spies who betray their countries into four types. One is the *Emily,* or the person born in the target country who is recruited and trained by an enemy agent. A second category is known as the *Mickey* (also called the "walk-in)," who, because of his or her job, has access to classified information, and thus "walks in" to a foreign intelligence agency and offers to spy for them. A third type, the *Philby* (named after British-intelligence-agent-turned-Soviet-spy, Kim Philby), is recruited in his or her youth, while living outside the target country, emigrates to the target country, and under a cover job, spies while living in the target country. Fourth, and finally, there are the *Willies,* or spies who are actually working for an enemy government intelligence service, but who are led to believe by the person who recruits them that they are working either for their own government, or for another organization, such as a credit investigation agency.

An example of a "Willie" case occurred in 1952, when a Washington newspaper columnist received an anonymous letter from a State Department employee giving confidential information about the State Department's harsh treatment of employees who were accused of having Communist sympathies. The newspaper columnist's chief investigator, in reality a KGB agent, discovered the letter-writer's identity and, unknown to the columnist, approached the person and offered to pay him for furnishing weekly reports of State Department "injustices."

The KGB agent told the employee that some of his patriotically inspired letters would be published as "a source close to the State Department," while the rest would be filed away as background material for other newspaper stories. Instead, the KGB agent sent the unpublished "background material" to his contact in the Soviet Union. Thus the State Department employee became a "Willie"—an intelligence agent who does not know he or she is an agent.

A consolation for the United States when victimized by such spies is the "need to know" policy, which states that employees—including the CIA director—when handling top secret material are allowed to know only what they need to in order to perform their jobs.

In spite of the CIA's skilled spying techniques, certain problems in intelligence gathering are inherent in an open, democratic society like that of the United States. One involves the availability of intelligence in America compared to the unavailability of intelligence in such totalitarian countries as the Soviet Union. For example, in the United States, for a small fee, anyone can write to the Government Printing Office to get information about such U.S. military capabilities as harbor installations and locations of U.S. airfields. And, technical magazines such as *Bulletin of Atomic Scientists* reveal the latest achievements in U.S. atomic research.

In April 1960, Vice Admiral Hyman G. Rickover, known as

the "father of the atomic submarine," told the Joint Atomic Energy subcommittee of Congress that a toy company had manufactured such an accurate model of the Polaris atomic submarine that "a good ship designer can spend one hour on that model and tell he has a million dollars' worth of free information."[5] Part of the model's instructions read:

> *This ballistic-missile firing nuclear submarine is . . . built in strict accordance with specifications contained in official U.S. Navy blueprints . . . the atomic reactor . . . and two Polaris missiles . . . are authentic in every detail. . . .*[6]

Admiral Rickover went on to say, "If I were a Russian I would be most grateful to the United States for its generosity in supplying such information for $2.98."[7]

While Soviet scientists routinely visit U.S. atomic installations, the Soviets are highly secretive about their atomic plants, hiding them under elaborate cover names. The Soviet equivalent of America's Atomic Energy Commission, for example, is the "Ministry of Medium Machine Building."

In addition, democratic legal processes in the United States present obstacles to prosecuting foreign espionage agents. One obstacle is the requirement of a public trial, which makes the government reluctant to prosecute, as testimony about U.S. national security would become public knowledge.

A second obstacle is the three-year statute of limitations, which prevents prosecution if the spy is caught three years after he or she commits espionage. A spy can be tried after three years only if his or her crime is punishable by death. The 1953 Rosenberg Law helped the situation somewhat by removing the statute of limitations in cases affecting national security, and making the death penalty possible for peacetime espionage as well as wartime.

A third obstacle is diplomatic immunity, which prevents punishment of foreign diplomats for crimes committed in the United States. This gives such diplomats the knowledge that they will not have to stand trial if caught, which gives them an incentive to spy. As it stands now, the State Department usually declares the accused diplomat *persona non grata*, meaning unacceptable, in the United States, and requires the diplomat to leave the country within a specified time period.

From its creation in 1947 until the 1970s, the Central Intelligence Agency steadily gained power and authority. Then in 1973, congressional investigations into alleged CIA abuses, such as eavesdropping on American citizens and its covert operations in such places as Cuba, Vietnam, and Chile, forced the CIA to curtail its power. CIA Directors James R. Schlesinger and William Colby, under Presidents Richard Nixon and Gerald Ford, cut back on espionage operations, reduced the number of agents employed, and placed more emphasis on technological intelligence, such as satellites.[8]

By 1980, the CIA staff had been cut by 50 percent, and undercover operations had been reduced from an average of 300 a year to fewer than 20. In addition, new laws were passed that prohibited surveillance of U.S. citizens unless they were believed to be engaged in criminal acts.[9] Toward the end of the 1980s, however, because of the many espionage operations discovered against the United States during the decade, there was growing concern that an overreliance on spy gadgets at the expense of human spying threatened future U.S. intelligence capabilities.[10] A case in point was that of Ronald Pelton, a former employee of the National Security Agency, who sold the Soviet Union classified information concerning U.S. capabilities to intercept and decode Soviet communications.

With espionage exposures like Ronald Pelton's weighted against CIA abuses, such as eavesdropping on U.S. citizens' phone conversations, troubling questions are raised. How much power should the CIA have? Should spy organizations threaten a free society? Should spies only gather information, or should their jobs include manipulating foreign governments as well?

According to the National Security Act of 1947, the CIA's main function is to gather secret intelligence, but it may also carry out "certain duties and functions in the intelligence field in addition to those specifically enumerated in the law."[11] In the 1970s, CIA officers claimed they spied on Americans because they needed to keep watch on people who might be compromised

The Making of an American Spy: What the CIA Is All About

by contacts with Communist countries, and that covert operations are vital if America is to survive against enemies who use these tactics against the United States.

CIA opponents argue that such spying on Americans and covert operations in foreign countries allow the CIA to become an invisible government. By law, the CIA reports to the President and the National Security Council, with the President making the final decision on all important intelligence operations. In addition, congressional "watchdog" committees check on the activities of the CIA. Yet committee members admit they do not like to question CIA operations for fear national security secrets will leak out of their committees and become public knowledge. And, as the Iran-contra scandal proved, CIA officers do not always tell the truth to these committees, nor apparently is the President always informed about CIA operations.

Concerns about the CIA's power and secrecy are compounded by the fact that the effectiveness of the agency remains unclear, since, to protect national security, we usually hear only of the agency's failures, not of its successes. In addition, to protect itself from criticism, and to preserve its secrecy, the CIA practices what is called plausible deniability. This practice—used by all intelligence organizations—means denying responsibility for any embarrassing or failed operation when there is even a 1 percent chance of being believed.

For example, President Eisenhower used plausible deniability in 1960 when an American pilot, Francis Gary Powers, was shot down over the Soviet Union while flying one of America's U-2 spy planes. Eisenhower denied that Powers was engaged in a spy mission until Powers himself confessed. In 1986, when American pilot Eugene Hasenfus's plane was downed over Nicaragua and weapons discovered aboard, the Reagan administration at first denied that the United States was assisting the contras.

While these arguments about the CIA's power persist, the agency carries out its intelligence business. Every day a CIA officer arrives at the White House carrying a document marked "The President's Daily Brief." What is inside that document remains a secret.

3
The Making of a Russian Spy: What the KGB Is All About

In June 1977, Robert Toth, a *Los Angeles Times* correspondent in Moscow, was arrested for accepting an envelope from a Soviet scientist that supposedly contained state secrets. After four days of KGB interrogation, and angry protests from the United States, Toth was finally released and permitted to leave the Soviet Union.

It is thought that the Soviets arrested Toth to protest President Jimmy Carter's support of human rights activists in Russia, by means of American journalists' reports about Soviet harassment of these dissidents. Toth's scientist friend had promised to give him articles on parapsychology. Instead, the Soviet Union, through the KGB, planted "state secrets" in the envelope. Whether the scientist was forced to go along with the deception, or whether he was a KGB agent assigned to trick Toth, or whether in fact, Toth was a CIA agent, is not known.

Planting evidence on someone the KGB wants to arrest, harass, expel, or even murder, is so common a tactic in Russia that Americans visiting or working there are warned never to meet a Soviet citizen alone, and never to accept a package from anyone if the contents are not clearly visible. In 1986, *U.S. News & World Report* correspondent Nicholas Daniloff became the twenty-eighth American correspondent expelled from Moscow since 1955, after he, too, was arrested for accepting an envelope containing "state secrets."

In spite of Soviet Premier Gorbachev's new policy of *glasnost*—meaning more openness about goings on in the Soviet government, and more freedom for Russians in general—the

Los Angeles Times correspondent Robert Toth and his wife Paula view a May Day Parade during their 1977 stay in Moscow.

KGB is still a secret police force that uses deception, torture, and assassination to achieve its goals.

How was the KGB created, and how did the Russian intelligence agency get so much power? Intelligence organizations in the Soviet Union are separated into two divisions—a military branch and a security branch. Both are controlled by the Soviet Communist party Central Committee and the Council of Ministers. The Russian military intelligence organization is the Chief Military Intelligence Directorate of the Ministry of the Armed Forces, (GRU) and is headed by the Minister of Defense. The

GRU is made up of the general staff of the armed services, and is responsible for running spy operations in other countries, and for collecting information about foreign armed forces and military installations.

The security intelligence organization of the Soviet Union is the *Komitet Gosudarstvennoi Bezopastnosti* (KGB), or Committee of State Security. The KGB has had several different names since its creation as the Cheka (Extraordinary Commission Against Counterrevolution And Sabotage) after the 1917 Bolshevik Revolution. The Cheka was a secret, terrorist police force that murdered anyone suspected of anti-Bolshevik activities. Secret assassination has continued to be a function of the Soviet security services.

When Lenin, the leader of the Revolution, died in 1924, one of his followers, Leon Trotsky, tried to gain control of the Communist party, but was defeated by Joseph Stalin. Trotsky went into exile in 1929, and for the next ten years was the chief target of the millions of Soviet assassinations ordered by Stalin. On August 21, 1940, the secret police found their mark, and Trotsky was murdered with an Alpine climber's ice-ax.

Under Stalin, the Cheka became the GPU, the OGPU, the NKVD, and the MGB. Stalin used the secret police, headed by Lavrenti Beria, to execute everyone he did not trust or like, and expanded its power to arrest, condemn, and execute Soviet citizens without a trial. After Stalin's death in 1953, and the selection of Nikita Khrushchev as premier, Beria himself was executed.

On March 13, 1954, the Soviet Council of Ministers changed the MGB into the KGB. Khrushchev took away many of the KGB's powers in a de-Stalinization program, which included prohibiting secret trials of Soviet citizens. Strengthening of the KGB began again when Yuri Andropov took it over in 1967. Andropov upgraded the standards for agents to be accepted into the KGB, and modernized its ways of gathering intelligence. As a result, the KGB lost its strong-arm image of being run by unintelligent Russian thugs dressed in baggy suits. Today's KGB agents are well educated and socially skilled. The KGB, which has branches in all fifteen Soviet republics, has its headquarters

The Making of a Russian Spy: What the KGB Is All About

on Dzerzhinski Square in a Moscow compound near the Kremlin. Loitering in the area is a cause for arrest, and even walking by the compound is regarded with suspicion.

The KGB is divided into several directorates, each with a different responsibility. The Third Directorate, for example, is responsible for maintaining security in the armed forces by watching out for potential defectors. This Directorate is believed to encompass SMERSH (*Smert Shipionam,* meaning Death to Spies), which author Ian Fleming portrayed as SPECTRE in his James Bond novels.

The Second Directorate of the KGB controls domestic repression, and thereby touches the life of every Soviet citizen. Countless informers work in every apartment building, office, factory, and school, all backed by an electronic surveillance system. The Fifth Directorate deals with dissidence and political crime, including torture and exile of Russian dissidents; the Seventh Directorate handles surveillance of major Moscow embassies; the Eighth develops encoding and decoding systems; and the Ninth guards party leaders.

To most people, the KGB means spies. It is the First Directorate that manages Soviet spies, controlling at least 10,000 KGB agents abroad, 500 of whom are believed to be in the United States. Soviet spies operate under the cover of diplomats, Aeroflot Airline staff, members of trade delegations, and correspondents for Soviet news organizations. Some spies are "illegals," agents who assume fictitious foreign identities to melt into the society on which they spy. Others are Americans recruited to spy for the Soviet Union, such as the John Walker family spy ring, exposed in 1985, who netted the Russians about one million documents on U.S. naval codes and submarine operations.

The First Directorate also handles sabotage, assassinations, and terrorist training. Its up-and-coming subdivision is Directorate T, responsible for stealing scientific intelligence. Russian technology theft has replaced other forms of espionage as the Soviet's number one goal. Their major target is the U.S. aerospace industry, involved in research for President Reagan's Strategic Defense Initiative, better known as "Star Wars."

Like the CIA's "need-to-know" policy, lower ranking intelligence agents are never told anything that could endanger the Soviet Union. They receive no special training, and their capture is usually ignored by the Soviets. A position with the KGB is much sought after however, as Soviet intelligence officers are considered the elite of Russian society. They are given special apartments, cars, private telephones, servants, dachas (houses in Moscow suburbs), their own club buildings, and the freedom to travel.

Moscow Center controls resident agents, and specific permission must be obtained from the Center to change any orders relating to an espionage operation, including where drops are to be located in foreign countries. The Center even controls the model of cars its agents can buy, and the brand of motor oil used in those cars.

In recruiting prospective KGB agents, the Soviet Union is said to have compiled the most complete name file in the world, gathered by Communist parties in over fifty countries. Facts included in these files are prospective agents' political affiliations, interests, family backgrounds, personal habits, quirks, and weaknesses. In comparison, the CIA uses a computerized filing and indexing system to keep track of suspected Soviet agents. U.S. computers rapidly translate Russian text into English. For example, the thousands of pages comprising the novel *Gone with the Wind* can be translated into Russian in five minutes.

To help assure that its agents are trustworthy, the KGB insists on three generations with no dissidents or blemishes in an agent's family. Before marrying, prospective KGB agents, like prospective CIA agents, are known to look up their fiances' records to be sure there is no incriminating information on them.

In addition, the KGB controls intelligence services of Soviet bloc or satellite countries. These include Poland, Hungary, Czechoslovakia, Albania, Yugoslavia, Bulgaria, and Rumania. The KGB keeps tabs on its satellite intelligence services by placing its own agents in the top jobs of these services, and by recruiting satellite intelligence officers to send back information on their operations and personnel.

The Making of a Russian Spy: What the KGB Is All About

While a KGB officer is given privileges and power, if he makes a mistake he may be demoted, imprisoned, or even executed. Soviet intelligence officers possess disciplined, merciless attitudes about following rules. During World War II, for instance, when the sister of General V.S. Abakumov, a high-ranking intelligence officer, was arrested for dealing in the black market, the police asked Abakumov how to proceed. He reputedly answered, "Why do you ask me? Don't you know your duty? . . . Shoot her."[1]

In most cases, Soviet citizens do not apply to become intelligence officers, but rather are chosen by their superiors in their regular jobs. Intelligence officers are given military ranks, even if they are not in the Soviet army.

Soviet agents usually begin their careers by being assigned to a secret police force in an outlying area of the USSR where they are not natives. At first their primary duties involve handling informants, who are local citizens who report anyone expressing disloyalty or criticism of the Soviet Union. While the agents are at this post, they receive training in espionage and counterespionage techniques.

After this assignment, KGB agents are transferred to intelligence headquarters in Moscow until they are deemed experienced enough to be transferred to a foreign country. If agents do not succeed in gathering much information in the foreign country, they are reassigned to their former posts outside Moscow.

The "Philby"-type KGB agents first live in the target country, learning its language and customs, and may even become citizens of that country. Their families do not go with them, as "making over" an entire family would be too costly and time consuming. The agent may assume the identity of a person of foreign birth, but must not be recognizable as a Russian or an Eastern European. In true James Bond fashion, the agent's passport and official documents might be those of a real person who has died.

The career opportunities for Soviet intelligence officers far exceed those of ordinary Soviet citizens, as a skilled agent can be appointed to a top-level position in the Communist Party. Yet the totalitarian government of the Soviet Union can serve as a disadvantage for its agents as well. For while serving in a foreign country, agents are exposed to the very comforts and freedoms the Soviet Union seeks to curtail. This love of "the good life" has caused many KGB agents to defect.

The KGB's recruitment procedures are often carried out in a cloak and dagger style. One method is entrapment, which is essentially blackmail. These potential agents either have already done something they would not want their families or bosses to find out about, or they are enticed by KGB agents into performing such an action. In many cases the compromising act is adultery or promiscuous sex. Entrapment usually involves inviting the potential agent to a social gathering, where that person's particular vice or temptation is offered. These potential agents' "taking the bait" is often videotaped or recorded, after which they are confronted with the "evidence," and told that unless they work for the Soviets, the incriminating evidence will be made public.

Some KGB agents are recruited from among Soviet refugees and exiles living in foreign countries. These refugees may be told that if they do not spy against their adopted countries, their families still living behind the Iron Curtain in the Soviet bloc will suffer. At other times, the refugee will receive a letter from family members saying local authorities are being harsh on them, but the situation could improve if the refugee would help the Soviet government.

Today, under the direction of Viktor Chebrikov, the KGB is employing strong-arm tactics that have not been seen since Stalin's days. The KGB now instigates subversive activities; directs border troops; controls wiretaps, censorship, and forgeries; investigates crimes; runs the prison system; and manages labor, immigration, and deportation. In addition, a rash of new laws has given the KGB even greater control over Soviet citizens. It is now a crime, for example, to put up foreigners overnight or to give them a ride in a car. A new ban on passing "official secrets" to foreigners has made Soviet citizens hesitate to talk to anyone about their work.

As correspondent Nicholas Daniloff noted: "KGB agents are, at least initially, polite and correct. However, they are not above planting evidence or organizing entrapments to get their man."[2]

The Making of a Russian Spy: What the KGB Is All About

Many Russian authorities believe the KGB will use its power to control not only Gorbachev's *glasnost*, but the entire Communist Politburo as well. With more than half a million spies at its disposal, the idea does not seem farfetched.

4

The Atom Spies: Espionage in the 1950s

In 1924, in New York City, the first Soviet espionage base was established in the United States under the cover of the Soviet trade agency Amtorg. From then until 1938, Russian spying on America was done with virtually no interference by the U.S. government. Soviet agents came into the United States on false passports. Members of the American Communist party helped these spies penetrate all areas of U.S. economic and political life. During World War II, for example, one Russian spy network infiltrated the OSS so completely that the Soviets knew the date of D-Day, the Allied invasion of Normandy, four days in advance.

One reason why Soviet espionage originally did so well in America was that during World War II, the USSR was considered an ally. A lend-lease policy had been established between the United States and the Soviet Union, whereby Russian technical experts and government officials were given practically whatever they asked for in goods, blueprints, and technological information.[1]

Victor Kravshenko, an official with the Soviet Purchasing Commission in the United States, described the results of lend-lease. "We transferred to the Soviet Union . . . dozens of tons of [atomic] material . . . by Soviet ships that came from lend-lease. . . . Who cared what we took? Had we taken the Empire State Building and put it on a ship, no one would have cared. . . ."[2]

In 1945, however, with the exposure of Communist spy rings in America, U.S. enthusiasm for lend-lease deteriorated. One

In 1948, Whittaker Chambers testified before the House Un-American Activities Committee in Washington.

spy was Whittaker Chambers, an avowed American Communist, who confessed he had been spying for the Soviets since 1930. Chambers turned over hundreds of secret documents unearthed from his Maryland farm, hence their name "Pumpkin Papers," which he said were given to him by former Assistant Secretary of State Alger Hiss and by other members of an underground Communist spy ring.

The spy exposure that caused perhaps the final blow to America's belief in Russia as an ally occurred in September 1945, when Igor Gouzenko, a Russian cipher clerk at the Soviet embassy in Ottawa, Canada, defected to the West. Gouzenko brought

SPIES AMONG US

with him more than one hundred notebooks and documents describing a vast Soviet international espionage network that had been in operation since before World War II. The ring's purpose was to steal atomic secrets from the West. Efforts by the FBI, the CIA, and Britain's SIS to capture the "atomic spies," as they were soon called, lasted well into the 1950s and, some intelligence experts claim, continue today.

In one of Gouzenko's notebooks was the name Alan Nunn May, a British physicist. In March 1946, Dr. May, code named "Alek," was arrested in England for violating Britain's Official Secrets Act. He confessed to having given the Soviet Union uranium samples being tested for use in atomic weapons. Dr. May's exposure motivated the FBI to take another look at the suspicious cases it had on file, which Whittaker Chambers had supplied in 1945. The FBI especially rechecked the file on former Assistant Secretary of State Alger Hiss who had also been an adviser to Franklin Roosevelt at the Yalta conference.

Meanwhile, in America, another Soviet defector was "opening the bag" on Russian spy operations. On November 8, 1945, Elizabeth Bentley, an employee of U.S. Service & Shipping, Inc., in New York City, confessed to the FBI that she had been a Soviet courier for the past decade. Bentley identified more than eighty Communist agents operating four espionage rings in the United States. She said thirty-seven of these agents, including Harry Dexter White, chairman of the International Monetary Fund, were U.S. government employees. She also confirmed the allegations of Whittaker Chambers against Alger Hiss.

In 1949, Judith Coplon, a U.S. Justice Department worker, was arrested for giving the Russians FBI reports about investigations on Communist espionage in the U.S. She became the first American civilian ever tried for espionage. Her conviction was later reversed, however, because the FBI had failed to obtain a warrant for her arrest. Shortly thereafter, a law was passed requiring no warrants in arrests involving national security.

By 1950, Americans were convinced the Soviet Union was about to overthrow the U.S. government, something they had been trying to do since 1917. Whereas before World War II, the

Elizabeth Bentley also testified in 1948 House Un-American Activities Committee hearings, identifying more than eighty Communist agents in key posts.

Communist party was legal in the United States, by the 1950s U.S. citizens were prosecuted for membership in the party, and the word "Communist" became synonymous with "Russian spy." The House Committee on Un-American Activities, led by Senator Joseph McCarthy, held hearings to question alleged members of the Communist party. McCarthy said the State Department was "thoroughly infested with Communists."[3]

McCarthy's fanatical determination to ferret out every person who had ever been connected in any way with Communism launched hysterical spy hunts in America reminiscent of the witch hunts in Salem, Massachusetts, in the 1600s. McCarthy's voice echoed across television screens and newspaper headlines with the now-famous question: "Are you now, or have you ever been, a member of the Communist party?" When witnesses took the Fifth Amendment, intended as a protection against self-incrimination, it came to be seen by some as proof of treason.

The testimony of Whittaker Chambers and Elizabeth Bentley about Alger Hiss matched Igor Gouzenko's statement that an assistant to the U.S. secretary of state was a Soviet agent. Yet there was insufficient evidence to try Hiss on espionage charges. However, in January 1950, Alger Hiss was convicted on the lesser charge of perjury for testifying to the House Un-American Activities Committee in 1948 that he was not a member of the Communist party and had not given classified documents to Whittaker Chambers. Hiss said he agreed to testify in order to clear himself of any wrongdoing. "I soon learned it wasn't that kind of committee," he later declared.[4]

The country was divided over the Alger Hiss case. Some people believed Hiss's claim that he was a victim of the FBI's determination to discredit President Franklin D. Roosevelt's liberal policies by tying them to Communist espionage. Paroled in 1954, Hiss has never stopped searching for FBI evidence that will prove his innocence.

The Senate Internal Security Subcommittee, led by Republican Senator William Jenner, was formed to expose Communist office holders in the Democratic Roosevelt and Truman administrations. The Jenner Committee reported that evidence provided by FBI files showed that Soviet spies had penetrated top-level positions in the government, and had stolen thousands of diplomatic, political, military, scientific, and economic secrets.

Meanwhile, another name that had been scribbled in Igor Gouzenko's notebooks was that of physicist Klaus Fuchs, a German-born, naturalized British citizen. From 1943 to 1946, Dr. Fuchs had worked with British and American scientists on the top secret Manhattan Project at the Los Alamos, New Mexico, atomic research center. The scientists were working on the separation of uranium isotopes by a process known as gaseous dif-

The Atom Spies: Espionage in the 1950s

fusion. The result would produce the world's first nuclear weapon, the atomic bomb.

At this point, four other "atomic spies" entered the drama. They were Harry Gold, a Philadelphia biochemist, David Greenglass, an ex-Army sergeant working as a machinist at Los Alamos, and the husband and wife who would cause an international furor that continues today—Greenglass's sister and brother-in-law, Ethel and Julius Rosenberg.

According to Harry Gold (code named "Raymond"), his Soviet contact, Anatoli A. Yakovlev, the Soviet vice-consul in New York, told him to meet Klaus Fuchs in Santa Fe, New Mexico, on June 2, 1945. Fuchs would give Gold information about the designs of the plutonium and atomic bombs, the gaseous diffusion process, and the implosion lens mold triggering device used to detonate the bomb. Gold was then to get drawings of the lens mold from David Greenglass.

Yakovlev allegedly gave Gold a piece of paper on which was typed the password, "I come from Julius," and Greenglass's name and address in Albuquerque, New Mexico. Yakovlev also gave Gold a torn section of a Jell-O box to give to Greenglass as identification. Greenglass would have the other half of the torn Jell-O box.

Gold's follow-up on the Greenglass meeting would become one of the major controversial points in the later trial of Greenglass and the Rosenbergs. At the trial, Gold testified that when he drove to Albuquerque to pick up the lens mold drawings, the Greenglasses were out for the evening, so he spent the night in a tourist home. The next day, Sunday, June 3, he allegedly checked into the Hilton Hotel, then returned to the Greenglasses' house. When a dark-haired young man answered the door, Gold said, "I come from Julius," and presented his half of the Jell-O box. David showed Gold the matching half, then gave him the sketches. Gold boarded a train that evening and arrived in New York Tuesday evening June 5, in time to see Yakovlev at their prearranged 10:00 P.M. meeting.

On August 6, the first atom bomb in history was dropped on Hiroshima, and on August 9, a second and more powerful atomic bomb was dropped on Nagasaki. Klaus Fuchs returned to England and went to work at the atomic research center at Harwell, where he continued supplying the Soviets with atomic secrets. Fuchs's method of contacting Soviet agents in England seems right out of the pages of a spy novel. Holding two books in one hand, and five books bound with string and suspended from two fingers of the other hand, Fuchs went to London's Paddington station at 8:00 P.M. on the first Saturday of the month. There, he would meet a man carrying the book *Try and Stop Me*, by the American book publisher and newspaper columnist Bennett Cerf.

In the summer of 1949, the Soviet Union exploded its first atomic bomb. British counterintelligence experts found evidence that the Russians had been getting highly specialized atomic information for some time. The trail led to Harwell and to Klaus Fuchs. He was arrested on February 3, 1950. Fuchs confessed, saying he betrayed his country because, "I had complete confidence in Russian policy, and I believed the Western allies deliberately allowed Russia and Germany to fight each other to the death. . . ."[5] He was sentenced to fourteen years in prison, the maximum allowed in England for giving secret information to an ally.

Fuchs told British intelligence that he had given his information to a fat, foreign-looking American who wore blue pin-striped suits, and who was known to him as "Raymond." The FBI reviewed photographs of people who had appeared before the New York grand jury in 1947–1948 for questioning about their Communist affiliations. Among the photographs, the FBI found a fat, foreign-looking American. He was Harry Gold, whom Elizabeth Bentley had also named as a coconspirator in her Soviet espionage ring.

The FBI secretly took films of Gold, and sent them to Klaus Fuchs in prison in England. Fuchs identified Gold as his Soviet contact. Harry Gold was arrested on May 15, 1950. At the time, he was wearing a blue pin-striped suit. Gold eventually confessed and implicated David Greenglass, whom the FBI arrested on June 15 in New York, where he was working as a machinist. Greenglass also confessed and agreed to turn state's evidence in

The Atom Spies: Espionage in the 1950s

return for a lighter sentence. He claimed the instigator of the spy ring was his brother-in-law, Julius Rosenberg.

Rosenberg, a tall, scholarly looking man with wire-rimmed glasses, had been a Communist since his membership in the Young Communist League while attending the College of the City of New York. He graduated as an electrical engineer in 1939 and married Ethel Greenglass, also an avowed Communist. David Greenglass idolized Julius, and he and his wife Ruth soon became Communist sympathizers. Four weeks after David Greenglass's arrest, the Rosenbergs were listening to "The Lone Ranger" with their two sons, Robert, six, and Michael, ten, when twelve FBI men knocked on their door. They arrested Julius and Ethel, who denied they were Soviet spies.

One of Julius Rosenberg's college classmates that the FBI interviewed was Max Elitcher, an engineer in the Navy Department. He claimed Julius had tried to induce him into joining his espionage ring by saying Elitcher's best friend, Morton Sobell, was among the scientists who were giving atomic information to the Soviet Union. In August, the FBI moved in on Morton Sobell.

The trial of the Rosenbergs, David Greenglass, and Morton Sobell began on March 6, 1951, in New York. The government's main witnesses were Max Elitcher, Harry Gold, who had already been sentenced to thirty years in prison, and David Greenglass. When her brother began his testimony, Ethel's face paled, and she hung her head. David never once looked at his sister while he spoke.

According to Greenglass, in November 1944, Julius Rosenberg told Ruth Greenglass that "David is working on a secret weapon called the atomic bomb. I want you to ask him to give me specific information about the locations, the personnel, and the experiments conducted at Los Alamos."[6] In January 1945, while on furlough in New York, David claimed that Julius asked him for sketches of what he was working on at Los Alamos. Julius allegedly then gave David the torn half of the Jell-O box to identify anyone who came to Los Alamos for more information from him.

In addition, Ruth Greenglass testified that Ethel told her,

From left to right, Morton Sobell, Julius Rosenberg, and Ethel Rosenberg leaving a New York City courthouse in 1951, shortly before their trial ended

"Julius has finally attained the ambition of his life—to be an undercover man in part of the Soviet espionage system in the United States. . . ."[7] Ruth said that David agreed to give her the information Julius requested, which she memorized, and Ethel Rosenberg typed up for delivery to Yakovlev.

The Rosenberg trial lasted thirty-one days. On March 29, 1951, the jury returned guilty verdicts against all four defendants. On April 5, Judge Irving Kaufman sentenced David Greenglass to fifteen years in jail; Morton Sobell to thirty years; and Julius and Ethel Rosenberg to death in the electric chair.

52

5
More Atom Spies: The Aftermath of the Rosenberg Trial

When Judge Kaufman sentenced the Rosenbergs to death, he said: "Deliberate, contemplated murder is dwarfed in magnitude by comparison with the crime you have committed . . . your conduct in putting into the hands of the Russians the A-bomb . . . has already caused . . . the Communist aggression in Korea . . . and who knows but millions more innocent people may pay the price of your treason."[1]

An appeal was immediately drawn up by the Rosenbergs' attorney, Emanuel Bloch, on the basis that perjured testimony had been used to convict the Rosenbergs, mainly that of Harry Gold. The original execution date of May 21, 1951 was postponed to allow the courts time to study the case.

In August, American Communists, who had ignored the entire Rosenberg trial, suddenly turned the case into a major propaganda campaign against the United States. Editorials in the Communist *Daily Worker* charged the U.S. government with a frame-up, claiming, since the Rosenbergs were Jewish, that the prosecution concocted evidence in an anti-Semitic witch hunt. Judge Kaufman's answer to the charge was to quote Emanuel Bloch's statement after the jury's verdict: "I feel satisfied by reason of the . . . questions asked during the course of your [the jury's] deliberations that you examined very carefully the evidence and came to a certain conclusion."[2]

All over the world doubt was created as to the Rosenbergs' guilt. By December, a National Committee to Secure Justice in the Rosenberg Case was created. During the next two years, the date of execution was postponed four times while seven petitions for review were sent both to the U.S. Circuit Court of Appeals and to the Supreme Court. When those failed, an appeal for clemency was sent to President Dwight Eisenhower, who sided with the courts. The final execution date was reset for Monday, June 15, 1953. Over 6,000 people, including the Rosenbergs' sons, marched outside the White House, carrying signs urging President Eisenhower to commute the death sentence.

Emanuel Bloch tried one last appeal, based upon a 1925 act of Congress, which stated that a justice may grant a stay of execution if a new point of law is presented that he regards as substantial. The Rosenbergs' attorneys thought they had found a new point of law—that the Rosenbergs had been tried under the wrong law. They were sentenced to death under the Espionage Act of 1917, under which the death penalty could be imposed for espionage committed in wartime. The attorneys claimed that the 1917 Espionage Act was canceled out by the Atomic Energy Act of 1946, under which a death sentence could be imposed only upon the recommendation of the jury. The Rosenberg jury had made no such recommendation.

Supreme Court Justice William O. Douglas agreed that a new point of law had been presented, and issued a stay of execution. On Thursday, June 18, the Supreme Court was called into special session to review the new point of law. The dissenting justices said, however, that the Constitution prohibits passage of an ex post facto act, meaning a law in which people can be prosecuted for crimes committed before the passage of a law against their crime. Thus, since the Rosenbergs committed espionage before the 1946 Atomic Energy law was passed, they could not be prosecuted under that law. Justice Douglas argued, however, that "Where two penal statutes may apply . . . the court has no choice but to impose the less harsh sentence . . . I know deep in my heart that I am right."[3]

In the end, the Supreme Court voted five to three against the appeal. The execution was reset for Friday, June 19, 1953, at 8:00 P.M. In the United States, executions are usually carried out at 11:00 P.M. However, because the Rosenbergs were Jewish,

As far away as France, there was strong feeling that the Rosenbergs had been unfairly sentenced to death. The sign here urges the crowd to "Save the Rosenbergs."

the hour was moved up out of respect for the Jewish Sabbath, which begins at sundown on Friday.

Shortly before 8:00 P.M. Friday evening, the prison chaplain recited the Twenty-third Psalm as the Rosenbergs began their death walk to the electric chair. By 8:25 P.M., Julius and Ethel Rosenberg had been executed. They were the first Americans to be put to death for espionage by an American civil court in peacetime.[4]

The executions set off demonstrations around the world. A National Committee to Reopen the Rosenberg Case was formed, and 21 years later, in 1974, 3,000 people jammed New York's Carnegie Hall to hear discussions about reopening the case. At least 25 books have been written on the Rosenbergs, some upholding the verdict and others challenging the government's evidence. *The Implosion Conspiracy* (1973), by Louis Nizer, for example, concludes that the evidence supports the guilty verdict. In 1975, the Rosenberg sons, Robert and Michael, still believing in their parents' innocence, wrote their own book, *We Are Your Sons: The Legacy of Ethel and Julius Rosenberg*. After their parents' execution, the boys were adopted by Anne and Abel Meeropol, and became Robert and Michael Meeropol to keep secret their identities as children of convicted spies.

The pro-Rosenberg view was also presented by Miriam and Walter Schneir in their book *Invitation To An Inquest* (1965). One piece of evidence they question is Harry Gold's testimony about his trip on June 2, 1945, to Santa Fe, New Mexico. Gold claimed he registered at the Hilton Hotel just for the day, as he had to start back to New York that night to keep his prearranged June 6 meeting with Yakovlev. Then why, ask the Schneirs, did he register for a hotel room he would not need?

The FBI claimed they obtained Gold's registration card from the Hilton Hotel. The Schneirs argue that the card was forged to prove Gold was in Albuquerque on June 3. The Schneirs discovered that the June 3 card, although dated June 3 on its face, had been time-stamped June 4 on the back. Hotel officials said the time-stamp would be the accurate record, the day Gold claimed to be on his way back to New York.

According to the Schneirs, tapes of Gold's statements to his lawyer did not match his courtroom testimony. For example, in his trial testimony, Gold said that Yakovlev gave him a piece of paper with Greenglass's name and address on it, and the recognition signal, "I come from Julius." Yet in the recorded interview with his attorney, Gold never mentioned the Greenglasses by name, but referred to them as "the GI and his wife," and said

More Atom Spies: The Aftermath of the Rosenberg Trial

he introduced himself to the GI by "the name of Mr. Frank, possibly Raymond Frank. . . ."[5] He did not mention the password, "I come from Julius," or the torn Jell-O box. At one point in the interview, Gold's attorney specifically asked him how he identified himself to "the GI." Gold answered, "it was something [like] Bob sent me or Benny sent me or John sent me. . . ."[6]

Two other major questions in the Rosenberg trial have been the value of the atomic information the Rosenbergs allegedly gave the Russians and the accuracy of the lens mold sketch David Greenglass said he drew for Julius Rosenberg. Dr. Walter Koski, David's boss at Los Alamos, testified that Greenglass's sketch was "substantially an accurate representation. . . ."[7]

In 1966, however, Dr. Philip Morrison and Dr. Henry Linschitz, two other scientists involved in the atomic bomb project, gave sworn affidavits that David Greenglass's sketch was a childish rendition and could not have helped the Russians make an atomic bomb. Moreover, they claim that America possessed no atomic secrets for the Rosenbergs to steal, as the theory behind the release of atomic power was known to scientists around the world, and it was only a matter of time before other nations would duplicate the atom bomb.[8]

And Dr. Edward Teller, a key developer of the hydrogen bomb, wrote in *The New York Times Magazine* on November 13, 1960, that "I believe the Russians could have produced an atomic bomb explosion without information from spies . . . there is probably no major scientific development of which the Russians are ignorant. . . ."[9] Finally, a report by the Joint Congressional Committee on Atomic Energy stated that the most damage caused by all the atomic spies "may have advanced the Soviet atomic energy program by eighteen months."[10]

In spite of the contradictory testimony given by Harry Gold, and the differing opinions about the value and accuracy of the atomic information given the Russians, it must be pointed out that the defense could have attempted to discredit the prosecution's testimonies by cross-examination or by calling in witnesses to refute their testimony. The defense took neither course of action.

If the Rosenbergs were indeed victims of a frame-up, it must be asked why the United States would build a fraudulent case against innocent people in the first place? The motivation might be found in the spy hysteria of the times. The House Un-American Activities Committee hearings fostered scare headlines that the Russians had stolen our atomic bomb with the help of American Communist traitors. Three 1950 headlines from *The New York Times* illustrate the spy hysteria atmosphere: "Atom Bomb Shelters For City At Cost Of $450,000,000 Urged"; "If Soviets Start War, Atomic Bomb Attack Expected In New York First"; "Gallup Poll Majority Favors Death For Traitors."[11]

As the foreman of the Rosenberg jury, Vincent Lebonitte, later said: "In my time a Communist was a monster, someone who was going to destroy me and my way of life. . . ."[12] Another member of the Rosenberg jury, Howard Becker, recalled that, "The defense and the judge said that Communism was not on trial, but I started to get the impression that Communism was on trial . . . after all, the Communists were out to overthrow the government."[13]

There was more fallout from the atom spy ring case when it was learned that in 1950, Bruno Pontecorvo, an Italian-born, naturalized British citizen, had given the Russians information on nuclear reactors, the devices used to make plutonium, thus providing the missing information the Soviets needed to make an atomic bomb. Before he could be indicted, however, Pontecorvo fled to Moscow. Then, in 1957, Jack and Myra Soble, leaders of another Russian spy ring, were indicted for having transmitted national defense secrets to the Soviet Union since 1941. Unlike the Rosenbergs, however, the Sobles pleaded guilty to avoid a possible death penalty.

The atomic spy ring's exposure led American government officials to realize the sobering fact that with regard to national security secrets, the question was not how well the secret could be kept, but for how long. Acting on this fact, Congress passed the so-called Rosenberg Law, which made peacetime espionage punishable by death, and eliminated the ten-year statute of limitations on crimes involving espionage that affects U.S. national security.

More Atom Spies: The Aftermath of the Rosenberg Trial

Today Julius and Ethel Rosenberg are still remembered either as the "spies who stole the atom bomb and gave it to the Russians," or as innocent victims of a witch hunt for Russian spies. While the controversy persists, Julius and Ethel Rosenberg lie in an unquiet grave.

6
Spies by Land or by Sea: Espionage Exposures in the 1960s

During the 1960s, the exposure of so many double agents and defectors on both sides of the Iron Curtain forced western and Communist intelligence agencies to overhaul their espionage branches and reevaluate their methods of operations. For example, in West Germany, the Gehlen Organization discovered in July 1963 that three of its agents, Heinz Felfe, Hans Clemens, and Erwin Triebel, had stolen 15,000 photographs of classified material for their Soviet contacts in East Berlin. Ironically, shortly before their arrest, General Gehlen had given Felfe and Clemens citations for ten years of meritorious service.

In the Soviet Union, meanwhile, three high-ranking KGB officers defected to the West, and "blew" countless Soviet intelligence operations. One of the defectors was Anatoli Dolnytsin, who "went over" to Great Britain in 1962. Among the information Dolnytsin gave British intelligence was evidence that led to the arrest of William Vassall, a clerk in the naval attaché's office at the British Embassy in Moscow, on charges of spying for the Soviet Union.

In England, a major British espionage exposé began in May 1961, when George Blake, a British intelligence agent working in West Berlin, was convicted of having spied for Russia for the past nine years. In 1955, Blake was posted in West Berlin by MI6, where he was to look for possible defectors among Red Army officers stationed in East Germany. Instead, Blake gave the KGB information about the joint CIA-SIS Berlin Tunnel, which had been dug from Rudow in the American sector of Berlin, to

Spies by Land or by Sea: Espionage Exposures in the 1960s

the suburb of Alt Glienicke in the Soviet sector. The tunnel tapped the Soviet cable network and attached it to an underground listening post, allowing Western agents to monitor messages between East Berlin and Moscow. By learning of the tunnel's existence, the KGB was able to send wrong information to the West.

Blake, who had also given the Soviet Union the organizational plans of MI6 and the names of its directors, confessed that, "There was not any official document of any importance to which I had access which was not passed to my Soviet contact."[1] By revealing these names, Blake caused the failure of many British espionage operations and the death of forty-two British intelligence agents. He was sentenced to forty-two years in prison, one year for each of the lives he had caused to be lost.

On October 22, 1966, when George Blake had served five and one-half years of his prison sentence, he escaped. Since Blake surfaced in Moscow a year later, it is believed the Soviets arranged his escape, with the help of Sean Bourke, a fellow prisoner of Blake's who had been released earlier that year. The escape, with its cloak and dagger style, was like a scene in a spy movie.

On the night of October 22, Bourke parked his car near the prison wall and got out. He held a flowerpot sprouting a long-stemmed carnation, inside of which was a two-way radio. Blake had previously been smuggled a similar radio. Pretending to smell the carnation, Bourke notified Blake when the "coast was clear," then tossed a rope ladder over the wall. Blake climbed the rope and jumped over the wall to the other side. Bourke drove him to an apartment, where Blake hid until the search for him was ended three months later. Then Bourke installed a false floor in the bottom of a van. With Blake hidden between the floorboards of the van and its false bottom, Bourke drove out of England to his final destination in East Germany.

Usually when an important spy is caught, the intelligence agency in question tries to arrange a prisoner swap to get the valuable spy back. However, these arrangements can take years to complete, as intelligence agencies frequently oppose such exchanges after having spent so much effort trapping the spy only to have him or her freed so quickly. Therefore, in the case of

George Blake, some intelligence experts claim the KGB decided to take a short cut and spring Blake from prison instead. As of 1986, Blake was reported to be alive and well and living in Moscow.

For the British, Blake's exposure left a lingering suspicion within the SIS that other Soviet agents had penetrated British intelligence. In the United States, the Blake case damaged the CIA's opinion of the SIS as inpenetrable, and resulted in strained relations between the two agencies. The CIA reasoned that the KGB had not stopped at infiltrating the SIS, but had penetrated other western intelligence agencies as well.

Another newsmaking spy scandal revealed in England during the 1960s was the Portland naval secrets case. It began in 1945, when Harry Houghton, a member of the British naval attaché's staff in Warsaw, Poland, became involved in black market dealings in antibiotic drugs. Unknown to Harry, his illegal activities were being monitored by both the Russian and Polish secret police for use as future blackmail to get him to spy for the Communists.

Twelve years later, in fact, when Harry was working as a clerk at England's Portland naval base, where he handled classified documents about research on electronic antisubmarine technology, he was approached by a member of Z-11, Poland's secret police. Harry was told that if he did not give Polish intelligence copies of these classified documents, his superiors would learn of his black marketeering.

When Harry refused to cooperate, Z-11 agents beat him up on his way home from work one night. From then on, Harry cooperated. Harry's Russian contact was a high-ranking Soviet intelligence agent who would become one of the most important Soviet agents captured by the West since World War II. He was Conon Molody, who was posing as Gordon Lonsdale, a Canadian who had been killed during World War II. Lonsdale told Harry that whenever he wanted a meeting, he was to mark in chalk the word "ox," with two lines drawn underneath on a wooden gate in a London park. Then the two would meet at the Maypole tavern on the first Saturday of the month.

At this point, MI5 started investigating Harry. He had been

Spies by Land or by Sea: Espionage Exposures in the 1960s

falsely accused of sending a hate letter to a photographer employed at Portland. During the investigation, MI5 learned that Harry's standard of living was considerably higher than his salary afforded. Harry was put under surveillance, and MI5 noted that he and another man often met on Waterloo Road, where Harry would hand the man a parcel. Sometimes Harry's girlfriend, Elizabeth Gee, who also worked at the Portland naval base, would accompany him. The stranger would deliver the parcel to a cottage in Ruislip, a London suburb.

On the morning of January 7, 1961, Harry, along with Elizabeth, who carried a large shopping bag, arrived by train at Waterloo Road and began walking down the street. A car pulled up to the curb, and Lonsdale jumped out. He took the shopping bag from Elizabeth, and the three continued walking. MI5 agents and Scotland Yard police, who had been tailing the couple, surrounded them. Inside the shopping bag was found a roll of film taken of a classified pamphlet titled, "Particulars of British War Vessels."

The three were arrested for violating the Official Secrets Act and taken to Scotland Yard for questioning. "To any questions you might ask me," Lonsdale said, "my answer is 'no,' so you need not trouble to ask."[2] He then refused to speak another word.

When Scotland Yard police went to the cottage in Ruislip, they found Helen and Peter Kroger, an American couple also posing as Canadians. In reality they were Morris and Lona Cozen, two American Communists linked with the Rosenberg spy ring who had fled the United States when the "atom spies" were caught. The Krogers were masquerading as antique book dealers while running a secret communications network between Moscow and London, either by short-wave radio or by microdots sent in the mail. A search of the Krogers' house turned up a wealth of spy gadgets, including a short-wave radio, a glass slide bearing three microdots, a cipher sheet, and a letter from Lonsdale to his wife in Moscow.

In March, the Portland Five, as they were called, were found guilty of conspiracy to commit espionage. Lonsdale was sentenced to twenty-five years in prison, Helen and Peter Kroger to twenty years each, and Harry Houghton and Elizabeth Gee to fifteen years each.[3]

One month later, events began taking place that would lead to Lonsdale's release from prison in a spy exchange with Britain. In November 1960, Colonel Oleg V. Penkovsky, a Russian official involved with Soviet scientific research, and who said he was disillusioned with the corruption of Soviet leaders, grew obsessed with the fear that Khrushchev would launch a nuclear war as soon as he felt capable of winning. Therefore, Penkovsky offered to spy for Britain for the good of the Russian people.

From April 1961, until his arrest on October 22, 1962, Penkovsky gave both British intelligence officers and American diplomats in London almost 5,000 photographs of Soviet documents related to Russian missile developments and troop movements. Penkovsky's courier was Greville Wynne, a British businessman. Wynne would visit Moscow on business trips, where Penkovsky would give him the documents hidden in boxes of chocolate. Through Wynne, Penkovsky told the West about the construction of the Berlin Wall, and the presence and location of Russian nuclear missiles in Cuba.

It was Penkovsky's information about the missile sites that caused his exposure. After the failed Bay of Pigs invasion, Khrushchev told President Kennedy that the Soviet Union would now supply Cuba all the arms necessary to repulse armed attacks. President Kennedy needed to know if he would set off a nuclear war by giving Khrushchev an ultimatum to either dismantle the Cuban missiles or face American retaliation. The answer was supplied by a radio message from Penkovsky in Moscow: "Soviet nuclear forces not in a state of war readiness."[4] Penkovsky added that the missile gap between the Soviet Union and the United States was in America's favor.

Kennedy thus gave Khrushchev his ultimatum, and the premier agreed to dismantle the Cuban rocket sites. Penkovsky, however, realizing the importance of a quick response, had not taken the usual security precautions in sending his message. The Soviet secret police picked up the message and arrested him. Penkovsky became the first Russian citizen since World War II to be publicly tried and convicted as a spy for the West.

Oleg Penkovsky grips the courtroom rail as his sentence to die in front of a firing squad is read out.

Oleg Penkovsky implicated Wynne as his courier, and in November, Wynne was kidnapped by KGB agents in Budapest, Hungary. Penkovsky and Wynne were tried jointly in May 1963. During the prosecution's summation, spectators in the courtroom were already reading copies of the summation in the Russian newspaper *Izvestia*, which had also already printed the sentences of the two men—death to Penkovsky, and ten years in prison for Wynne. *Izvestia* was only slightly off. Wynne received eight years, and Penkovsky was shot by a firing squad. One of Penkovsky's greatest blows to the Soviet Union was that he revealed details about Russian espionage operations in other countries, which caused the Soviet Union to cancel these operations and recall a considerable number of its intelligence agents stationed abroad.

Even before the Penkovsky-Wynne trial was over, however, the Soviets hinted they would like to trade Wynne for Gordon Lonsdale. When the British intelligence service opposed the exchange, the Russians used Wynne's poor health to change MI5's mind. Wynne's wife had been sending him packages of vitamins for his ulcer. The Russians refused to give Wynne the vitamins, and when his health had deteriorated considerably, they invited Mrs. Wynne to visit her husband in Moscow. Upon returning to London, she pleaded with the government for help. Believing Wynne would die if left in the Soviet Union, the British Cabinet voted to exchange Greville Wynne for Gordon Lonsdale.

Thus, shortly after five A.M., on April 22, 1964, two Mercedes-Benz cars, one black and one yellow, crept through the foggy dawn into the Heerstrasse crossing point, the area dividing the western and Russian sectors of Berlin, called "no man's land." Greville Wynne got out of the yellow Mercedes, Gordon Lonsdale the black one, and they switched cars. And two more spies came in from the cold.

The exchange was criticized by some British officials as setting an unequal precedent. They reasoned that every time the Russians wanted to get one of their spies out of a British jail, they would merely arrest a British citizen in Russia on phony espionage charges and hold him for exchange. A postscript to the Portland

Spies by Land or by Sea: Espionage Exposures in the 1960s

naval secrets case occurred in July 1969, when Britain traded Helen and Peter Kroger for Gerald Brooke, a British schoolteacher arrested in Moscow for giving the British coded instructions for receiving Soviet radio signals.

Meanwhile, in the United States during the 1960s, the CIA suffered two major espionage defeats. One was Moscow's discovery of America's U-2 spy flights over the Soviet Union in May 1960. The other was the failed Bay of Pigs invasion of Cuba in 1961. Afterwards, President John Kennedy ordered a reorganization of the CIA and appointed John A. McCone to become its director, replacing Allen Dulles, who had served in this position for eight years. More CIA changes occurred in January 1962, when the agency's headquarters was moved from an office building in downtown Washington, D.C., to a modern complex of buildings atop a bluff in Langley, Virginia, ten miles west of Washington.

In June 1963, another embarrassing blow to U.S. security occurred with the discovery that Stig Wennerstrom, a Swedish military attaché in Washington, had been giving the Soviets microfilmed information on U.S. technological advances. Before his exposure, Wennerstrom had been so highly thought of by U.S. government officials that he had been given the Legion of Merit. At embassy parties, his favorite way of passing microfilmed documents was to leave the microfilm in his coat pocket, which he checked on a numbered hanger when he arrived. He secretly told the number to his Russian contact, who then retrieved the microfilm from Wennerstrom's coat pocket.

In 1965, Robert Glen Thompson, thirty, a former U.S. Air Force clerk, was sentenced to thirty years in prison for giving the Russians photographs of U.S. secret documents while stationed in West Berlin in 1957. Thompson's motive was revenge against his commanding officer, who had once caught Thompson in civilian clothes and needing a shave, and had become enraged at him. Thompson insisted he was a patriotic American in spite of his spying. "I still get the flutters when they play the 'Star-Spangled Banner,' if that means anything," he said.[5]

The Russians, however, apparently believed Thompson's true

loyalty lay with them, since they gave up two jailed western spies in exchange for Thompson in 1978. Freed were an American college student, Alan Van Norman, who had been arrested in 1977 for attempting to smuggle an East German family into West Berlin; and an Israeli citizen, Miron Marcus, twenty-four, who had been jailed in Communist Mozambique for eighteen months after bad weather forced him to land his private plane there while on a flight to South Africa. Mozambique troops claimed Marcus was spying on Soviet and Cuban activity in Mozambique and reporting his findings both to the CIA and Israel's Mossad.

In 1968, the United States was back in the news with a blockbuster spy scandal reminiscent of the U-2 flight exposure. This time, however, instead of a spy airplane, the vehicle was a ship named the *Pueblo*.

The *Pueblo* was one of more than eighty ELINT (electronic intelligence) ships the U.S. Navy uses as a counterespionage force to the Soviet's spy ships, which are primarily made up of converted fishing trawlers. Just as U.S. "spook ships" prowl international waters off China, North Korea, and the Soviet Union, so Russian trawlers patrol waters off the coasts of California, South Carolina, Florida, Guam, and Alaska. The primary mission for the fleets is the systematic collection and classification of submarine "signatures"—the electronic blend of propeller and engine noises, wake turbulence, and magnetic fields generated by each individual sub. These "signatures" can be analyzed to locate enemy submarine positions.

Shortly after noon on January 23, 1968, the *Pueblo*, on its first spy mission, was fired upon and captured by North Korean gunboats. Fireman 3/c Duane D. Hodges was killed, and ten of the crew, including the ship's commanding officer, Lloyd M. Bucher, were wounded. Quickly, the crew started to shred, burn, or dump all classified documents on board and to hack up the electronic intelligence gear. However, the North Koreans swarmed aboard before the destruction was completed. They forced the *Pueblo* to sail into the port of Wonsan, where the eighty-two surviving crewmen were transported to a prison in the North Korean capital of Pyongyang.

Numbers on this photo of the captured *Pueblo* indicate the many devices available for electronic intelligence gathering.

The *Pueblo*'s orders specifically stated that "the closest point of approach" to Korean shores "will be 13 nautical miles."[6] The North Koreans claimed the *Pueblo* had sailed beyond the three-mile limit into their territorial waters. While negotiations were going on for the crew's release, the men of the *Pueblo* were undergoing interrogation and torture by their captors. The crew was so badly beaten that, in order to save their lives, they signed false confessions saying they were spies and made phony statements denouncing U.S. foreign policies.

Finally, after eleven months of negotiations, the United States signed a confession dictated by North Korea, and, with North Korean knowledge, at the same time released a denial of that confession. State Department officials later explained the North Koreans would use the confession for propaganda purposes in allied countries without broadcasting the denial of the confession. Thus, on December 22, 1968, the *Pueblo* crew was released.

The week before their release, the crew had been beaten severely when the North Koreans discovered a trick the men had played on them. Shortly after their capture, the Koreans had taken a photograph of the crew, which was circulated worldwide to show how "well treated" the prisoners were. In the photo, several of the crew made obscene gestures with their fingers.

On January 20, 1969, the crew appeared before a Navy board of inquiry in Coronado, California, to answer some troubling questions: Why didn't Commander Bucher fight back? Why hadn't the crew destroyed the electronic gear and the ship before its capture? And what made the crew sign the false confessions and denunciations of U.S. policy?

Some members of Congress believed the men had acted in a cowardly manner. Georgia Senator Richard Russell said at the time: "These men . . . are heroes in the sense that they survived the imprisonment. But they did sign a great many statements that did not reflect any great heroism in my mind. . . ."[7] Other U.S. officials, however, supported Bucher's conduct. Secretary of Defense Robert McNamara pointed out that there was not enough time to destroy all the surveillance equipment on board or to rig explosives to destroy the *Pueblo* before the Koreans captured the ship.

Bucher testified that he did not attack the North Koreans because there were no U.S. attack ships or fighter planes within range of the *Pueblo* to help launch such an attack, and he was outnumbered by the Korean fleet. To explain why the crew signed false confessions, Bucher described the torture used by the North Koreans.

In one instance, he said the Koreans kicked him unconscious, then took him into the basement of another building where he awoke to see an allegedly captured spy with "a compound fracture

Spies by Land or by Sea: Espionage Exposures in the 1960s

in his right arm—the bone was sticking out. He had completely bitten through his lower lip. . . . His right eye had been put out. . . ."[8] The North Koreans told Bucher this is what would happen to him and his crew if they did not confess that they were spies. Bucher himself was kept in solitary confinement during the entire eleven months.

When the inquiry was concluded that May, Commander Lloyd Bucher was considered either a hero who chose to save his crew rather than sacrifice it or a skipper who betrayed Navy tradition, although the truth was probably neither. The Board of Inquiry recommended that letters of reprimand be sent to the *Pueblo*'s officers, and that Bucher and Lieutenant Stephen Harris, the Navy intelligence officer on board, be court-martialed for violating the 1955 Uniform Code of Military Justice. This Code states that if captured, one is bound to give only name, rank, service number, and date of birth, and swears to make no oral or written statements disloyal to the United States.

Secretary of the Navy John H. Chafee however, rejected the board's recommendation, saying that the *Pueblo*'s mission was based on the assumption that North Korea would not violate the principle of freedom of the high seas. Since that assumption was made at all levels of government, all had to share in the consequences. Meanwhile, Purple Hearts were awarded to the ten wounded crewmen.

The "Pueblo Incident" was officially closed, but some questions remain unanswered. One is whether confessions made as the result of torture should be against the Uniform Code of Military Justice. Given the beatings and torture suffered by the *Pueblo* crew, a second question is whether the intelligence gained by such peacetime spy missions is worth the cost in human lives.

7
Going Over to the Other Side: Spies Who Defect

> *Our virtual survival as a nation may well depend on our ability to attract defectors who can bring us military secrets and warnings of what is being plotted by Red Moscow.*
> Robert Morris, chief counsel, United States
> Senate Internal Security Subcommittee,
> November 10, 1957.[1]

In August 1960, William H. Martin, thirty-one, and Vernon F. Mitchell, twenty-nine, junior cipher clerks in the U.S. National Security Agency (NSA)—the intelligence agency responsible for electronic spy gadgets and secret codes—bought one-way plane tickets to Havana, Cuba, where they were then picked up by a Soviet trawler. Vernon and Mitchell had defected to the USSR.

They took with them documents describing the organizational setup of the NSA and a list of both Soviet and allied countries' secret codes that the NSA had broken. Later, at a press conference in Moscow, they said they defected because they believed the United States "secretly manipulates money and military supplies to bring about the overthrow of unfriendly governments."[2]

Not all defectors are spies. They may be soldiers, ballet dancers, Olympic athletes, or ordinary citizens. Yet convincing intelligence agents on the "enemy" side to defect is a major function of all intelligence organizations, and separate funds are kept available in all agencies just for this purpose. Defectors can provide up-to-the-minute information about their intelligence agency's espionage operations, training methods, and tactics, in addition to the names of double agents, called moles, in the intelligence

Going Over to the Other Side: Spies Who Defect

service to which they defect. Sometimes defectors are turned into moles themselves, continuing to work for their country's intelligence service while providing ongoing information about that service to the government to which they defect.

All intelligence agencies use people's weaknesses to persuade them to "come over to the other side." For example, the CIA might look for KGB officials who seem to enjoy the material luxuries afforded them outside the Soviet Union, who seem unhappy in their jobs, or who are addicted to alcohol, drugs, gambling, or money. Yet not all defectors are recruited. Some defect out of sheer necessity. Sometimes the necessity is that their espionage operation is on the verge of being exposed, as was the case with British intelligence officers Kim Philby, Guy Burgess, and Donald Maclean.

In Communist countries, when one regime is overthrown, the new regime often purges members of the old regime by firing them, putting them in prison, or executing them. In these circumstances, surviving previous officials or spies frequently defect to the West to save their lives. One such spy was the Russian Alexander Orlov, who defected to the United States in 1938 when Joseph Stalin came to power and started liquidating almost every KGB officer who knew about his past crimes.

When Stalin died in 1953, his secret police chief, Lavrenti Beria, was executed, and a purge of Beria's men began that lasted for two years. During this time, many Soviet intelligence agents defected to the West, including Vladimir Petrov, a cipher clerk at the Soviet Embassy in Canberra, Australia, and his wife, assigned to operational work under the KGB resident there. In April 1954, the Soviet ambassador in Canberra sent reports to Moscow accusing the Petrovs of trying to form a pro-Beria group of embassy officials. On this charge, the Petrovs knew they could be recalled to the Soviet Union and imprisoned.

Vladimir wanted to defect, but his wife was afraid her relatives in the Soviet Union would be harmed. Thus, without telling her, Petrov turned himself over to Australian authorities and gave them KGB documents he had stolen from the Soviet embassy. The Soviet ambassador convinced Mrs. Petrov to fly back to

Russia. Two KGB guards stood on either side of her and held her arms as they walked through the air terminal. People screamed at her not to leave, that once in the USSR she would surely be killed. The guards forced her to board the plane.

At a stopover between Australia and Moscow, however, an Australian official got Mrs. Petrov alone for a minute and asked if she wanted to stay in Australia. She answered yes, but she was afraid her husband was dead and feared for her relatives' safety in Russia. Minutes before the plane was due to take off again, Petrov phoned his wife at the airport and convinced her she would be killed if she returned to the Soviet Union. Mrs. Petrov chose to stay in Australia.

Defectors usually experience emotional turmoil, either frightened for the safety of their families left behind or unhappy about their exile from their native countries. While in this troubled state, the defector is barraged with questions from the intelligence agency to which he or she defects. Josef Frolik, a Czechoslovakian intelligence officer who defected to the West in 1968, wrote that, "Western intelligence officers want to know the names of officers, how you worked, how much you were paid, the operations, where you were recruited, even what the office looked like. I was talking, talking for about three years, five days a week, hours on end. . . ."[3] On the other hand, the CIA guarantees the defector housing, medical needs, and training for a new job.

While defectors can be an asset to an intelligence service, they can also provide startling or embarrassing information. For example, when Major Florentino Azpillaga, a member of the DGI, the Cuban foreign intelligence directorate, defected to the United States from his post in Czechoslovakia in June 1987, he gave the CIA names of many Cuban double agents who supposedly had been conducting espionage operations for the United States, but in reality had been working for Cuban President Fidel Castro. These agents had been feeding the CIA false or useless information for years. The misinformation had been used by the United States to analyze and establish U.S. foreign policy.

Sometimes defectors can prove to be liabilities for the intelligence agency to which they defect, often creating more problems than they solve. One reason is that training of intelligence agents has improved considerably over the years, with the result that a defector frequently will bring authorities secret documents and codes stolen from his government only to learn the other government already has those documents and codes. In this case, the defection would backfire, as the defector's government would assume the other government had the defector's information, and thus change the codes and procedures that were noted on the stolen documents.

A reason the CIA is not overly enthusiastic about most defectors from Communist countries is that they sometimes use defection as a cover to spy on western countries for the Communists. These people eventually redefect, claiming they are disillusioned with the West. The chance of giving asylum to a double agent is why the CIA views with suspicion any defector who "walks in," preferring to recruit defectors by bribery or blackmail. Two Soviet KGB agents whose defection to the West might be considered to have caused more harm than good were Yuri Nosenko and Anatoliy Golitsyn.

Defecting on December 22, 1961, Golitsyn claimed that the Soviet Union had flooded western intelligence services with KGB agents, or moles, and planned to take over western intelligence services. He warned that the Soviets had launched a disinformation campaign to convince the West that Communist bloc countries were split apart by dissension. The Communists then hoped they could take advantage of the West's relaxed attitude about the threat of Communist aggression.

If Golitsyn's story were believed, it would mean, for example, that the emergence of Solidarity in Poland as a protest organization against Soviet restrictions of human rights was in reality a smoke screen to hide a strengthening of Communists in Poland. The Soviet ruse could also mean the Russian dissident movement would have to be viewed as a KGB-sponsored front, making dissidents like Andrei Sakharov a loyal Communist and defender of the Soviet Union. On the plus side, Golitsyn's tips did help lead to the exposures as Soviet spies of British intelligence officers William John Vassall, Anthony Blunt, and Kim Philby.

Then, to make Golitsyn's testimony more unbelievable, in 1964 KGB officer Yuri Nosenko defected to the United States and claimed there were no moles in the CIA. The Agency split into three factions—pro-Nosenko, anti-Nosenko, and a faction that maintained there were no conflicts between Golitsyn's and Nosenko's information. One of the staunchest supporters of Golitsyn's story was James Jesus Angleton, who was CIA counterespionage chief at the time. In 1963, believing the Soviet moles were working in the CIA's Soviet bloc division, Angleton cut off that division from information about top secret cases, and a Soviet mole hunt ensued.

Critics of Angleton accused him of causing a standstill in the division's operations, while CIA officers with years of outstanding performance were investigated, and several careers were ruined. One CIA officer proposed that Golitsyn and Nosenko were part of a KGB plot to protect the chief Soviet mole within the CIA, whom they claimed was none other than James Jesus Angleton himself. While Angleton was never formally accused of espionage, he was believed to have caused unfounded suspicions between intelligence officers within the CIA. In 1974, believing Angleton's pursuits of a mole in the Agency were doing more harm than good, and eager to quell accusations of CIA spying on American citizens—a program which Angleton directed—CIA Director William Colby fired Angleton.

The result of the Golitsyn/Nosenko defections was that during the 1960s and early 1970s, the CIA's obsessive mole hunt hurt relations between western intelligence services and almost stopped the CIA's counterintelligence agents in the Soviet Union. No chief Soviet mole has ever been found.

As for western spies who defect to the Soviet Union, no one caused as much world-wide fascination, or as much harm to the SIS and the CIA, as British intelligence officer Harold Adrian Russell (Kim) Philby and his British intelligence officer cohorts, Guy Burgess and Donald Maclean.

Kim Philby spent thirty-four years as a Communist double agent. What made him "go over" to the Soviets is still a topic of debate today. Regarded by the British as the master spy of all

One of the most famous of recent spies, Harold "Kim" Philby, photographed in Moscow around 1955

time, Philby was surprisingly not the James Bond type. He stuttered terribly and, at times, drank to the brink of alcoholism. Ruthless in his espionage work, those who knew him well claim he personally was a warm and likeable man.

Kim Philby's defection to Russia began on the evening of January 23, 1963, when he failed to show up at a dinner party given by the secretary of the British Embassy in Beirut, Lebanon. His wife, Eleanor, thought perhaps Kim was off on a story, as he had always been secretive about his work as a journalist for two Beirut newspapers. The next morning, however, when Kim had not returned, the Lebanese secret police were notified. Yet in spite of searching all hospitals, jails, and departure records for Lebanese airlines and ships, the police found no trace of Kim Philby.

The next day, Mrs. Philby called off the search, having received a letter from Kim saying he was off on a news assignment. Yet Eleanor Philby could not help wondering why he had not taken any clothes with him or why the police had not discovered how he had left Beirut. Rumors abounded that Philby either had been kidnapped by British intelligence, abducted by the CIA, committed suicide, or fled to the Soviet Union. For he had been a high official in British intelligence.

Then Mrs. Philby received a letter from Kim with specific instructions: She was openly to buy airline tickets to London for herself and her three children, but to secretly pick up tickets to Prague, Czechoslovakia, which would be waiting for her at the Czech airline. The Czech flight would leave Beirut the same day and time as the London flight. Eleanor should board the Czech flight, and once on board, she would be told her final destination. The letter also told her how to contact Kim in an emergency. She was to place a flowerpot in her kitchen window, and a friend of Kim's would contact her.

How had the son of Harry St. John Bridger Philby, a famous British diplomat in India, become a Soviet agent? One explanation has been that Kim inherited his father's contempt for the British establishment and England's policies in the Middle East. Through observing his father's life—Harry had been an explorer of Arabia, and eventually become a Muslim—Kim may have developed a desire for daring experiences and a determination that his life would equal his father's.

In 1931, Kim enrolled in Trinity College, Cambridge University. The 1930s in England were years of unemployment, hunger marches, and fear and hatred of Fascism, which was rising along with Hitler in Germany. For many British intellectuals, antipatriotism, which comprised sympathy for the poor, pacifism, and hatred of capitalist inefficiency, was the popular political stance of the day. Communism (at that time meaning the ownership and distribution of property, products, and income by the community, rather than by individuals) was considered a respectable ideology by university students and other members of the educated elite. Membership in the Communist Party was thought to represent a stand against Fascism.

As the poet Cecil Day-Lewis said, "No one who did not go through this political experience during the thirties can quite realize . . . how radiant for some of us was the illusion that man could, under Communism, put the world to rights."[4]

Like many of his classmates, Kim Philby was concerned about the poor condition of the English working classes, and saw Communism as the way to give these people a better life. It is thought that he was recruited into the Communist Party at Cambridge, along with his two friends, Guy Burgess and Donald Maclean. Their recruiter is now believed to be Anthony Blunt, a fellow Cambridge student who served in British intelligence from 1940 through 1945. In 1964, Blunt was given immunity for secretly confessing to British intelligence that he had spied for the Soviets during World War II. Blunt, who died in 1983, was once asked why he betrayed his country. He replied, "Cowboys and Indians."[5]

Kim Philby graduated from Cambridge in 1933 and became a journalist until 1938, when he got a job in MI6 in charge of training British double agents to penetrate Communist intelligence agencies. Philby established a reputation for brilliance in his work and soon became head of MI6's counterespionage operations. In reality, Philby was working for Soviet intelligence and passed secret information to the USSR throughout World War II. Yet his conduct remained above suspicion, and he was awarded the Order of the British Empire.

By the end of the war, Philby had married his second wife. In 1949, he was transferred to Washington, D.C., as liaison officer on security matters between the SIS and the CIA. In Washington, Philby passed American secrets to the Soviets. In August 1950, Philby's Cambridge friend Guy Burgess was sent to Washington as second secretary of the British Embassy. In a few months, Burgess's behavior became hysterical. He was convinced the United States was about to enter a third world war, and he started expressing anti-American sentiments in written reports to England. As a result, the British ambassador asked Parliament to recall Burgess to England.

Before this request was answered, Philby found a report stating that the FBI suspected both Burgess and Philby's other Cambridge friend, Donald Maclean, of spying for the Soviet Union. Maclean had served in the British Foreign Office in Washington, where he had access to information about U.S. military tactics and positions in the Korean War. In April 1951, Kim told Burgess about the FBI report. Burgess immediately went back to England, where he told Maclean that the FBI was on to them. The two men secretly fled to the Soviet Union.

British intelligence questioned Philby about his role in the affair. His answer was that he had told Burgess about the report, because he believed it was ridiculous, since the FBI was known to make outrageous allegations. But when Burgess left the United States, Philby said he realized Burgess might indeed be a Soviet agent, and had immediately informed the British ambassador. British intelligence justified Philby's behavior on the grounds that anyone would have done the same for an old college friend.

The FBI and CIA, however, were not so willing to accept as innocent Philby's warning to Burgess. Then CIA Director General Walter Bedell Smith warned the SIS to "get rid of Philby or we break off liaison on secret matters."[6] The British, believing it was vital to maintain working relations with the CIA, called Philby back to England and fired him. Meanwhile, high-ranking members of the SIS, believing Philby really was the "third man" in the Burgess/Maclean spy network, decided to plant Philby in a job in the Middle East, hoping he would lead them to key members of the Soviet network in the Arab world.

It took SIS more than five years to arrange this setup. In the spring of 1956, a member of the British Foreign Office asked the editors of an English weekly, *The Observer*, to hire Kim as their Middle East correspondent. Meanwhile, the editors of another

Going Over to the Other Side: Spies Who Defect

English weekly, The Economist, also asked Philby to work for them. Thus, in September, Kim Philby moved to Beirut.

During Philby's first year in Beirut, he was put under "quiet surveillance," which meant his British and American friends in Beirut were told that Philby might have Communist connections and that any information they could supply about such connections would be appreciated. One of the Americans was Sam Brewer, the Middle East correspondent for The New York Times. Philby's wife had recently died, and relatives in England were taking care of their children. Soon Philby was having an affair with Brewer's wife, Eleanor. In the spring of 1958, Philby and Eleanor told Sam about their relationship, and she flew to Mexico for a quick divorce. Upon her return, she and Kim were married. They eventually had three children.

While in Beirut, Kim's newspaper articles never showed his Communist beliefs, but instead expressed fear of Soviet penetration into Arabia and the Persian Gulf. Many American diplomats considered him the best western journalist in the Middle East. By the fall of 1962, British intelligence began to think that if Philby were indeed a Soviet spy, he was on an inactive list. Then an incident occurred that changed their minds. Kim attempted to recruit an Arab politician into British intelligence, offering him a sizable amount of money. By coincidence, the Arab was *already* working for SIS, and reported Philby's approach to his case officer.

The SIS decided to place Philby under surveillance, with the help of the Lebanese secret police. It was discovered that Philby was turning up at odd addresses for secret meetings with suspicious characters. Twice he had been observed standing on the terrace of his apartment at night, constantly checking his watch, then finally waving a dark object in the air.

After an intensive search of the area, the police caught an Armenian who admitted receiving Philby's messages and passing them on to another intermediary. Unfortunately, the Armenian had no idea what the messages meant, and the police could not decipher them. The British asked the Lebanese to put the Armenian in prison for a while, to cut off Philby's line of communication and thereby force him to talk directly to his Soviet contact.

Almost a month later, Philby made this communication. Late one night he left his apartment, hailed a taxi, and went to a shabby apartment above an Armenian candy shop. An official of the Soviet Embassy joined him. The SIS decided to confront Philby with their suspicions. Although his answers were unsatisfactory, the British could not arrest him on foreign soil, nor could they ask the Lebanese to extradite him, as Philby had done nothing illegal in Beirut. On the night of the British Embassy dinner, on January 23, 1963, Kim Philby disappeared.

A witness was later found who had seen a man answering Philby's description board the Russian ship, *Dolmatova*, along with two heavyset men. The ship left Beirut on January 24, its destination Odessa in the USSR. On July 1, the British publicly announced that Kim Philby had been the "third man" in the Burgess-Maclean affair and that he had been a Soviet spy since before 1946. On July 30, the Soviet newspaper *Izvestia* announced that the Soviet Union had granted Philby political asylum. A short time later, Eleanor and their three children boarded the plane that took them to the Soviet Union, and to Kim.

What information did Kim Philby, whom British intelligence experts still consider the most devastating spy ever to infiltrate the SIS, give the Soviets? It is known that he told Moscow about the 1951 Anglo-American invasion of Albania aimed at toppling the Communist regime there. He thus was responsible for sending hundreds of English and American soldiers to their deaths, having arranged for them to be landed in Albania, only to be met by Soviet troops. Further, he most likely passed on personal and classified information about the weaknesses of leading western intelligence officials, western attitudes toward the Middle East, and political developments in Jordan and Saudi Arabia, where the USSR had no diplomatic missions. In addition, he recruited an unknown number of spies for the KGB.

In the United States, Kim Philby's exposure left behind an atmosphere of distrust and suspicion regarding British intelligence. FBI Director J. Edgar Hoover remained distrustful of the

Going Over to the Other Side: Spies Who Defect

SIS until his death in 1972. Former CIA Director Walter Bedell Smith informed the SIS that the CIA would not continue its special working relationship with British intelligence until it cleaned up its organization. The British, not wanting to lose the CIA's cooperation in international espionage cases, complied.

Guy Burgess and Donald Maclean eventually died in Moscow. Kim Philby wrote a book about his life as a Soviet agent, titled *My Silent War.* He eventually divorced Eleanor, married and later divorced Donald Maclean's wife, then married his fifth wife, a Russian woman. Until his death on May 11, 1988, at the age of seventy-six, Kim Philby lived in Moscow where he worked as a full colonel in the KGB. When asked if he would do it all again—and send countless Western agents to their deaths—Philby replied, "Absolutely."

8

In from the Cold: Swapping Captured Spies

A white line marks the halfway point on the Glienicke Bridge, an old iron girder that stretches from West Berlin to Potsdam, East Germany. In the cold, gray light of dawn on February 10, 1962, two groups of men, starting from opposite sides of the bridge, walk toward that white line. With their hands jammed deep inside their coat pockets and their hats pulled low over their heads, they hunch forward against the chilling fog.

No one speaks. The click of their heels hitting the pavement is the only sound disturbing the eerie quiet. The men stop at the halfway line and wait, their anxious breaths frosting in the cold air. Finally a command is given, and a man from the Eastern Zone switches sides with a man from the Western Sector. Someone from the western side pats the newcomer on the back and whispers, "You're home." And the exchange of convicted Russian spy Rudolf Abel for alleged American spy pilot Francis Gary Powers is completed.

To a casual observer, this scene might not attract much attention, but to players in the espionage game, the Abel/Powers spy swap was called the most unusual and significant prisoner exchange of modern times. One reason was that the exchange broke the time-honored, but unwritten, rule that if a spy is caught, the spy's government neither acknowledges the spy's existence nor admits knowing anything about any espionage operation. By arranging for the swap, the United States and the Soviet Union were in effect admitting that Abel and Powers were spies, and

In from the Cold: Swapping Captured Spies

that they had indeed carried out espionage operations for their governments.

For the United States, this was only the second time that such an admission had ever been made. The first was during the American Revolution, when Nathan Hale, disguised as a teacher, spied on the British. Now American newspapers compared Hale's last words before being hanged, "I regret that I have but one life to give for my country," to Powers's statement to his Soviet prosecutors, a plea for mercy: "I am a human being who has never had any charges brought against him in any court, and who is deeply resentful and profoundly sorry for what he has done."[1]

During negotiations for the exchange, further comparisons between the two men were highlighted. Rudolf Abel was described as a master spy. Abel's defense attorney, James B. Donovan, said that Abel "was an intellectual, a gentleman, and I found him fascinating."[2] Assistant U.S. Attorney General William F. Tompkins called Abel, "the very best spy we ever saw," but criticized Powers for his weak conduct while under Soviet interrogation, saying, "We gave them [the Russians] an extremely valuable man, and got back an airplane driver . . . it's like trading Mickey Mantle for an average ballplayer. . . ."[3]

When the two men's backgrounds are compared, there is perhaps a kernel of truth in Tompkins's remarks. For while Abel's background was sophisticated—linguist, photographer, electronics expert, and professional engineer—Powers had no experience with, and showed little interest in, any occupation other than flying, which was his passion.

The Powers/Abel swap started the practice of spy exchanges that continues today. Since the United States usually has in custody more Soviet agents than the Soviet Union has western agents in Russian prisons, the then CIA Director Allen Dulles predicted that "If the idea of swapping agent for agent becomes the practice, the Soviets will be anxious to have a backlog of apprehended agents in their hands. Hence they will . . . likely succumb to the temptation to arrest casual visiting westerners who have nothing whatever to do with intelligence."[4]

Dulles's prediction proved correct. One of the most glaring

examples occurred in September 1986, when *U.S. News & World Report* correspondent Nicholas Daniloff was exchanged for Gennadi Zakharov, a Russian scientist employed at the United Nations in New York. In a sting operation, Zakharov was arrested on August 23, 1986 while making a payoff for classified documents on a U.S. jet engine to a student from Guyana whom Zakharov had recruited to spy for the Soviets, but who was actually working for the FBI.

Seven days later, on August 30, Nicholas Daniloff was arrested by KGB agents in a Moscow park after a Russian acquaintance he knew as Misha handed him an envelope of newspaper clippings. The KGB said the envelope contained top secret photos and maps. Daniloff was the first American civilian to have been arrested in the Soviet Union since Powers. The United States considered his arrest a retaliatory action for the Zakharov sting. After intense negotiations, Daniloff was released to the American Embassy in Moscow on September 12, and on September 29 was officially exchanged for Zakharov. As in the Abels/Powers exchange, some U.S. officials criticized the swap as violating the fairly recent government policy of prosecuting spies not protected by diplomatic immunity.

Fallout from the case included a series of expulsions by each country of Soviet and American diplomats. The expulsions had started in May 1986, when President Reagan expelled twenty-five Soviet diplomats from their United Nations Mission in New York on spy charges. On October 19, the Soviets retaliated by expelling five American diplomats from the Soviet Union, charging them with carrying out "impermissible activities against the Soviet state."

The tit-for-tat expulsions continued on October 21, when the United States expelled 55 more Soviet diplomats from their missions in New York and San Francisco, in effect wiping out top KGB and GRU agents in the United States, and reducing the number of Soviet diplomats in the United States to the same number allowed in the Soviet Union—225 at the Moscow Embassy and 26 at the Leningrad Consulate.

In a final move, the Soviet Union, on October 22, expelled

Left, Gennadi Zakharov, and *below*, Nicholas Daniloff, two of the most newsworthy of recent "spy" exchange cases

SPIES AMONG US

5 American diplomats, withdrew 260 Soviet employees from the U.S. missions in Moscow and Leningrad, and declared that Russians could no longer work for U.S. diplomatic missions in the Soviet Union. In addition, any Americans sent to Russia to work as employees at U.S. missions there would count toward the 251 total of American diplomats allowed in the Soviet Union.

The Daniloff/Zakharov swap was achieved in record time compared to the Powers/Abels exchange, which was the final event in two espionage operations that had begun in the 1950s. . . .

Francis Gary Powers, from the rural town of Jenkins, Kentucky, had been a fighter pilot in the Air Force during the Korean War. In 1956, Powers took a job with Lockheed Aircraft Corporation in Burbank, California. The company's chief engineer, C. L. Johnson, had initiated a new test flight program to check the performance of airplane engines and electrical systems while flying at high altitudes. As part of the program, Johnson designed a plane capable of cruising for hours at 70,000 feet, while going 500 miles per hour. Johnson named the plane the "Utility 2," or "U-2" for short.

A danger of flying at high altitudes, however, is what pilots call "flame-out," when the thin air at these altitudes causes the engine to stall, due to insufficient oxygen to burn the fuel. When a flame-out occurs, the pilot has to drop 30,000 to 40,000 feet to restart the engine. The U-2's main disadvantage is that the kerosene fuel, needed to fly at high altitudes for long periods of time, is difficult to restart.

In 1955, the CIA was looking for a plane to be used for reconnaissance flights over the Soviet Union, in order to obtain information about Soviet missile capabilities. When the CIA learned that a U-2 test pilot, while flying at 50,000 feet, had taken photographs of a golf course in which two golf balls could clearly be seen on one of the links, the Agency knew they had found just the plane they needed.

A secret Air Force team known as 10/10 was formed to fly the U-2 missions which, for a cover-up, were said to be part of a worldwide weather research program conducted by the National

In from the Cold: Swapping Captured Spies

Advisory Committee for Aeronautics (NACA). NACA set up secret U-2 bases at Incirlik, Turkey, and Atsugi Airport near Tokyo.

The U-2s photographed missile sights in the Soviet Union by means of seven camera windows built into the bottom of the plane, through which wide-angled cameras took continuous pictures. To take a picture, the pilot merely pushed a button when flying over designated points. If detection by the Soviets occurred, the pilot pushed another button that activated a detonator to destroy the plane, but which operated on a timing mechanism so that the pilot could eject before the plane blew up.

Despite the CIA's efforts to keep the U-2 flights secret, Russian radar picked up the planes as they skirted the Soviet/Afghanistan border. In fact, only five months before Powers's plane was shot down, the Soviet air force newspaper, *Soviet Aviation*, reported that the American U-2 planes were being used for strategic reconnaissance.

In May 1956, Gary Powers was accepted into the CIA's U-2 program. In August, he was sent to the base at Incirlik. In case of an emergency on his U-2 flights, Powers carried a silver dollar that contained a needle with curare, a lethal poison. In addition, he carried a black cloth cut into a specified shape to identify himself when he landed at Bodoe Air Base in Norway after his mission. The cloth would match one held at the base, and thus would prove he was really Gary Powers, and not a Russian impostor flying his captured plane.

On May 1, 1960, at 5:36 A.M., Gary Powers took off for Sverdlovsk, to photograph a new Soviet rocket allegedly sitting on a launching pad there waiting to be tested. At 8:55 A.M., Powers's U-2 was picked up by Soviet radar as he crossed the Soviet/Afghan border, and Soviet antiaircraft planes were alerted. Due to thick clouds, Powers had difficulty orienting himself in relation to the ground. As he approached Sverdlovsk, the plane shook violently, and an orange flash sprang from the tail section—the signs of a "flame-out." Then, while gliding down to 30,000 feet to restart the engine, Powers used his emergency code, "Puppy 68," to radio for help.

SPIES AMONG US

Soviet antiaircraft missiles fired at his plane at the same time that U.S. tracking stations lost touch with him. Without pushing the "explosion" button, Powers bailed out and parachuted to the ground. Later, at his American trial, he said that when the plane began to fall down, he was pressed against the control panel and could not reach the "explosion" button to destroy the plane.

Powers landed near a farm twenty miles southeast of Sverdlovsk. He was spotted by Soviet police, arrested for espionage, and flown to Lubianka Prison in Moscow. At his subsequent trial, Powers confessed: "I plead guilty to the fact that I have flown over Soviet territory . . . and turned on and off the necessary controls of the special equipment mounted aboard my plane. This, I believe, was done with the aim of collecting intelligence information about the Soviet Union."[5]

While Powers was being shot down by the Soviets, the 10/10 detachment at the Bodoe Air Base in Norway notified Washington that Powers was in trouble. According to espionage tradition, Powers was a discovered, (blown) agent, and no acknowledgment of his existence could be made. Therefore, no search was ordered for his plane, and no news was released about his flight. Nevertheless, Powers's wife Barbara was told he was missing, and a search had begun. On May 5, Soviet Premier Khrushchev announced that an American U-2 plane had been shot down over Soviet territory, but did not say where, or whether, the pilot was still alive.

In response, the U.S. State Department, using the intelligence practice of plausible deniability, released a cover story that a weather research plane was missing, that the pilot had reported oxygen trouble, and therefore the plane may have accidentally strayed over Soviet airspace. But then the next day, Khrushchev announced that American pilot Francis Gary Powers was in Soviet custody. No longer able to hide behind plausible deniability, President Eisenhower announced that the U-2 flights were being operated to "gather . . . the information required to protect the United States and the free world against surprise attack and to enable them to make effective preparations for defense."[6]

Thus Eisenhower became the first American President to

Francis Gary Powers during his 1960 trial in Moscow

admit publicly that the United States carried on espionage operations. At a U.S.-Soviet summit conference held shortly afterwards, Khrushchev demanded that Eisenhower condemn the espionage act and promise to renounce such actions in the future. When Eisenhower refused, the Summit ended. On August 17, Powers was put on public trial in Moscow. He was sentenced to three years in prison and seven years in a labor camp. Under Soviet law, Powers's wife could join him there.

On February 18, 1962, *The New York Times* said that "The story of Francis Gary Powers may be a . . . humiliation to the Central Intelligence Agency, but . . . the more permanent damage has been done in the psyche of the American male whose romantic illusions about the nature of the secret agent have suffered a shattering betrayal. . . ."[7]

In comparison to Francis Gary Powers, Soviet spy Rudolf Abel, who was born in Moscow in 1902, had been well-trained in espionage practices. At intelligence posts throughout Europe, he learned to speak English and, although no one knows how, developed an Irish accent. During World War II, he served as an intelligence officer on the German front. In 1948, as a lieutenant colonel in the KGB, Abel immigrated to the United States through Canada. He settled in Brooklyn, New York, where he posed as an artist/photographer under the name of Emil Robert Goldfus. (After Abel was arrested, a check with the U.S. Department of Health showed that the real Emil Robert Goldfus had died on October 9, 1903, at the age of one year, two months.)

While living in Brooklyn, Rudolf Abel's neighbors never suspected he was a Russian spy, but rather considered him a model citizen, always paying his bills on time and keeping regular hours. When the CIA later searched Abel's apartment, they found a short-wave radio and an antenna strung from his window to a neighbor's roof, along with codes, maps, microdots, and photographs relating to U.S. disposition of armed forces and atomic energy. Abel had hidden the incriminating evidence in hollowed-out batteries, coins, pencils, and cuff links.

During the nine years Abel spent in the United States, his job consisted of recruiting spies and transmitting to Moscow the

In from the Cold: Swapping Captured Spies

information his network collected. One of Abel's favorite methods of sending these messages was to insert microdots in the bindings of American magazines, which he mailed to Soviet cover addresses in different European cities.

In 1952, Moscow assigned Reino Hayhanen to serve as Abel's assistant. The two men used dead letter drops, such as the inside of hollowed out screws located at the bottom of lampposts in Manhattan's Riverside Park; inside cracks in a cement wall in the Bronx; and behind a loose brick under a bridge near the Central Park reservoir. To indicate there was a message left in a drop site, they used such signals as blue chalk marks on subway stair railings. A horizontal mark meant a message was in the drop; a vertical mark meant a message had been picked up. One time Abel left a message inside a hole in a flight of stairs in New York City's Prospect Park. Before Hayhanen arrived to pick up the message, however, maintenance men cemented the hole. Years later, the FBI dug the message out of the stairs.

For a few years Abel and Hayhanen worked together in harmony. However, the KGB's choice of an assistant for Abel proved a grave error of judgment. By 1956, Hayhanen had become an alcoholic, and consequently he fell down on his espionage work. In addition, he was a thief, having kept $5,000 he was ordered to give to the wife of a convicted Russian spy. When Abel returned to Moscow on a vacation that year, he informed his superiors about Hayhanen.

In 1957, Hayhanen was recalled to Moscow "for a consultation." Aware of how the KGB "consulted" with its unsatisfactory espionage agents, Hayhanen traveled as far as France. Then on May 4 he walked into the American Embassy in Paris and defected. A week later he was flown to the United States, where he told FBI agents about Abel and their spy network.

Rudolf Abel's unmasking, however, is said to have begun even before Hayhanen's confession. According to legend, one afternoon in 1953, fourteen-year-old Jim Bozart, a Brooklyn newspaper boy, received fifty cents in change from a customer. "I was walking down the stairs," he said, "and the change slipped from my hand . . . when I picked it up, one of the nickels had

Rudolf Abel heads for court as his 1957 espionage trial begins.

split in half . . . one of them had a piece of microfilm in it. It was a picture of a . . . row of numbers. . . ."[8] Bozart gave the nickel to the police, who passed it on to the FBI. Experts were unable to decipher the numbers until Hayhanen gave the FBI the key to the code. The microfilmed message had been written by Abel to Hayhanen.

When Hayhanen did not show up in Moscow as expected, the KGB sent a warning to Abel, who promptly vacated his

In from the Cold: Swapping Captured Spies

Brooklyn apartment and rented a room at the Latham Hotel in New York City under the name of "Martin Collins." His attempt to hide was too late, however, as on June 21 the FBI found "Collins" in his hotel room and arrested him for entering the United States illegally. Thus ended the espionage career of Rudolf Ivanovich Abel, the Soviet Union's top spy in the United States.

As Abel was being escorted out of his apartment, he tried to slip a piece of paper up his sleeve. FBI agents confiscated the paper, which was a coded message consisting of five-digit numbers arranged in rows. In a wastebasket, agents found a hollowed out block of wood containing the cipher pad for the code and a pencil with a hollow eraser containing eighteen rows of microfilm, one of which was Abel's schedule for radio broadcasts to Moscow.

The FBI declared Rudolf Abel to be the greatest spy so far in the twentieth century. Using the code name "Mark," Abel had commandeered his spies so well that it is believed only one or two couriers even knew what "Mark" looked like. The CIA offered him $10,000 a year to become a double agent for the United States. Abel refused. Had he defected, all espionage charges against him would have been dropped.

His attorney, James B. Donovan, believed Abel's bond with his country, a feeling of "my country right or wrong," was what made him agree to become a Soviet spy in the first place, and then refuse to acknowledge he was a secret agent once he was caught. Abel admitted only that he was a Soviet citizen posing as an American and had illegally entered the United States. On November 15, 1957, Rudolf Abel was convicted of espionage against the United States. He was the first spy to be tried and convicted of espionage under the Rosenberg Law, which allows the death penalty if convicted of spying for a nation with which the United States is at peace.

In obtaining Donovan as his defense attorney, Abel received the first of two lucky breaks. Donovan urged the judge to give Abel a prison sentence rather than the death penalty, saying, "It is possible that in the foreseeable future, an American of equivalent rank will be captured by Soviet Russia . . . at such a time an exchange of prisoners through diplomatic channels would be considered to be in the best national interest of the United States."⁹ When Francis Gary Powers was shot down, Abel received his second lucky break.

Apparently agreeing with Donovan's reasoning, the judge sentenced Rudolf Abel to thirty years in prison and levied fines totaling $8,000. He was sent to the federal penitentiary in Atlanta, Georgia, where he was described as a model prisoner. In his free time he read and painted. One of his paintings was a portrait of President John Kennedy.

In June 1960, Gary Powers's father wrote Rudolf Abel in prison suggesting he write his government about a prisoner exchange between Abel and Powers. Abel asked Powers's father to contact Abel's wife in East Germany. In the fall, Donovan received a letter from Abel's wife asking for clemency for her husband. When John Kennedy succeeded Eisenhower in 1961, he believed the prisoner exchange would help foster better relations between America and the Soviet Union. *Newsweek* magazine, in its February 9, 1962, issue, commented on Kennedy's decision, saying, "The President felt . . . that the U.S. had got all it was going to out of Abel, and now it was important to know how much the Russians had got out of Powers."

In the meantime, the East German police had arrested Frederic Pryor, a twenty-eight-year-old American graduate student, on espionage charges. Donovan made a "package deal" with the Soviet Embassy in East Berlin to release Pryor and Powers in return for Abel. Thus, on Saturday morning, February 10, 1962, U.S. military police waited in a car parked on the western side of the Glienicke Bridge for word that Frederic Pryor had been released at the Friedrichstrasse crossing between East and West Berlin, more commonly known as "Checkpoint Charlie." When the release was confirmed via car radio, Abel and Powers changed places. After walking across the Glienicke Bridge, Colonel Rudolf Ivanovich Abel was never seen or heard from again by western government officials.

Many Americans were shocked by Powers's cooperation with his Soviet captors. Perhaps the main reason he did not put up more resistance was that he was not trained as a spy. Powers was

In from the Cold: Swapping Captured Spies

questioned by the Senate Armed Services Committee about his actions after being shot down. On March 6, 1962, he was declared not guilty of all misconduct charges against him.

On August 1, 1977, Powers, in his job as a helicopter pilot reporting weather and traffic conditions for KNBC television in Los Angeles, was flying back to Burbank, California, from covering a brushfire north of Santa Barbara. With him was cameraman George Spears. At 12:38 P.M., their helicopter crashed in a field near Encino. Both men were killed. Francis Gary Powers was forty-seven years old.

9

Of Spies and Satellites: Espionage in the 1970s

On March 2, 1978, twenty-three-year-old William Kampiles, an ex-CIA officer, stood watching the sun set behind the Tomb of the Unknown Soldier in Athens, Greece, when he felt a tap on his shoulder. Kampiles turned around, nodded to a man known to him as Michael, and gave him some papers. In return, Michael handed Kampiles $3,000, then rushed off to tell his superiors in the KGB that he had received the last pages of a top-secret CIA manual on the KH-11 reconnaissance satellite system.

From 300 miles above Earth, the KH-11 can take detailed photographs, even through clouds, of missile silos on the ground, then develop the pictures instantly—a major advance over earlier satellites that sent cannisters of film back to earth by parachute.

Shortly after William Kampiles left Greece, he did something that continues to puzzle the CIA. He went to CIA headquarters in Langley, Virginia, and told CIA officer George Joannides that, while pretending to still be working for the CIA, he had made contact with a Soviet agent in Athens who paid him $3,000 to deliver secret information to the Soviets. Kampiles now wanted to serve as a disinformation agent for the CIA, by giving misleading information to the Soviets.

At this point, Joannides should have realized that Kampiles's story was a lie, as it is known that the Soviets never pay for information *in advance*. Yet Joannides passed the matter along to his superior, and not until three months later was an investigation initiated. A CIA officer working in the Soviet section heard Kampiles's story and realized the man was lying. On August

In 1978 William Kampiles was found guilty of stealing a top-secret government document and selling it to a Soviet official.

17, Kampiles was arrested for espionage and theft of government secrets. He was found guilty and sentenced to forty years in prison.

The Kampiles case revealed laxity in CIA procedures for handling classified documents. For example, when the FBI asked the CIA if the manual was missing, no one at the agency knew. A record is kept of everyone who handles each top-secret CIA document, by having each such person sign a receipt. Yet there was no record of the person in the Watch Office to whom the manual was given. Neither could the officer who left the KH-11 manual in Kampiles's office remember to whom he had given it.

After the trial, more contradictory evidence surfaced concerning the exact date the KH-11 manual was first compromised (given to the Soviets). When CIA Director Stansfield Turner was called by the Senate Intelligence Committee to testify about the Kampiles case, he stated that the CIA first suspected information from the KH-11 manual had been leaked in July, 1978, four months after Kampiles sold the manual. Yet according to U.S. intelligence sources outside the CIA, the agency was aware of a leak concerning the KH-11 as early as August, 1977, and a secret security check had already begun to find the source of the leak.

Former CIA Director Richard Helms speculated that the CIA might have been penetrated by a top KGB agent, and Kampiles was being used as the "fall guy." According to this theory, the Soviets would originally receive information on the KH-11 satellite from an important and unsuspected Russian mole in the CIA. Then, unknowingly, Kampiles would steal another copy of the manual for the Soviets, so they could set him up to get "burned" (caught) by convincing Kampiles to tell his story to a CIA officer. This would lead to his arrest, and thereby protect the Soviet mole.

There is still speculation since the alleged mole's identity has yet to be discovered. Some intelligence officers claim the KH-11 was first compromised even earlier than August 1977, tracing the leak back to a spy operation exposed in 1976 that involved two "all-American boys" who decided to sell out to Moscow. One of the defendants confessed that "I turned over to the Soviets five to ten typed pages dealing with the . . . communications satellite . . . the type that flies daily over Russia taking photographs."[1] There was at that time only one satellite system capable of both communications and taking photographs. That system was the KH-11.

The exposure of this case began shortly before noon on January 6, 1976, when a young man attempted to toss a long pink

Of Spies and Satellites: Espionage in the 1970s

envelope over the wall surrounding the Soviet Embassy in Mexico City. Mexican police officers, who always keep the building under surveillance, surrounded the man and questioned him about the contents of the envelope. Instead of answering, the man offered the officers $500 to let him go. When the police refused, he dropped a marijuana cigarette on the ground and tried to hide it with his shoe. The police arrested the young man for possession of drugs.

The police inspector phoned Thomas Ferguson, a vice-consul in the American Embassy. Ferguson, whose job involved helping Americans deal with Mexican authorities, had handled many such drug cases, and was therefore not particularly disturbed by the call. When he arrived at police headquarters, however, and the inspector showed him photographs developed from film strips found in the young man's envelope, Ferguson got alarmed: the photographs were of dozens of classified CIA documents, all stamped "Top Secret."

So began the case that one CIA officer called "the most serious breach of national security in a decade,"[2] but is better known by the name reporter Robert Lindsey gave to the case in his book titled, *The Falcon and the Snowman.*

The young man taken into custody by the Mexican police was Andrew Daulton Lee, twenty-five. Ten days later, Lee's accomplice, Christopher Boyce, twenty-four, was arrested as he came home from hunting with his pet falcon. Raising birds was as passionate a hobby to Boyce as dealing cocaine was to Lee. Hence the 1979 book title *The Falcon and the Snowman.* For the past two years Lee and Boyce had been selling KGB agents information about the CIA's secret intelligence gathering operations at TRW, a U.S. defense contractor.

Lee and Boyce, two of the youngest Americans ever caught spying against the United States, seemed to be unlikely candidates for spies. They grew up in the wealthy residential area of Palos Verdes, California, they came from loving families, and had been altar boys in their Catholic church. Boyce's father was a former FBI agent, and Lee's a prominent pathologist. Lee, although not a good student, was popular, had played Little League baseball, participated in high school football and wrestling, and was a skilled table and cabinet maker.

In the late 1960s and early 1970s, when a drug culture was prevalent among America's youth, Andrew Lee followed along. By the time of his arrest for espionage, Lee was a full-time drug dealer who had already been arrested five times for possession and selling of drugs, three times for driving while intoxicated, and once for suspicion of robbery and resisting arrest. Lee was spending money faster than he could make it—sometimes, people said, to buy friends. He served seven months of a one-year jail sentence, then wrote to a judge begging to be released so that he could go to college. The judge consented. Lee enrolled in a junior college, but soon dropped out and started dealing drugs again. A warrant was issued for his arrest, and in 1975 he fled to Mexico.

Christopher Boyce, on the other hand, had never been in trouble before his arrest for espionage. Christopher was a brilliant student, with an IQ of 145, and was considered a model of good behavior. Yet he dropped out of college in 1974 and, through his father's connections with the FBI, got a job as a communications clerk with TRW, the CIA's major manufacturer of spy satellites. Some of these satellites could take live television pictures of foreign defense activities. Others, using infrared sensors, could pick up fiery emissions from enemy ICBMs lifting off toward America, thus giving the United States thirty minutes warning of a Soviet attack, and thereby time to counterattack with U.S. missiles.

Boyce was in charge of the code room at TRW, called the "black vault." He was one of eight men who had passed an intensive security investigation run by the CIA before he was allowed inside the vault. Besides "top secret" clearance, Boyce had been approved for "cryptoclearance," allowing him to handle coded material. His job was to transmit information, including coded messages from America's armed forces, about TRW's satellites to CIA headquarters in Langley, Virginia.

In 1975, while Boyce was working for TRW, Andrew Daulton Lee contacted the Soviet Embassy in Mexico City and offered

ESCAPED FEDERAL PRISONER

Originally Sentenced For Espionage (40 years)

NAME: BOYCE, Christopher John
DOB : 2-16-53
SEX : Male
HGT : 5'9"
WGT : 160
EYE : Blue
HAR : Brown
POSSIBLE HOBBY: Falconry

SMT : Mole left jaw.
POB : Santa Monica, CA
DOW : 1-21-80
RAC : White
SOC : 566-94-9235
FPC : 1604TT10031654TT0405
NCIC: W224966144

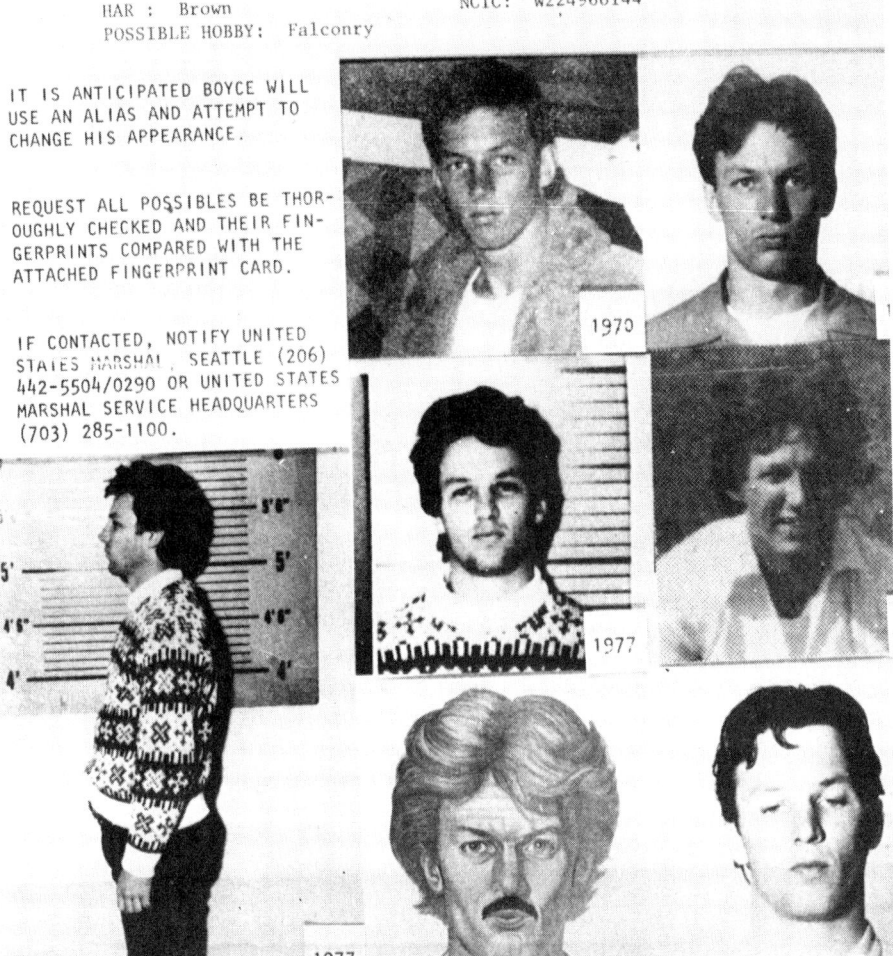

IT IS ANTICIPATED BOYCE WILL USE AN ALIAS AND ATTEMPT TO CHANGE HIS APPEARANCE.

REQUEST ALL POSSIBLES BE THOROUGHLY CHECKED AND THEIR FINGERPRINTS COMPARED WITH THE ATTACHED FINGERPRINT CARD.

IF CONTACTED, NOTIFY UNITED STATES MARSHAL, SEATTLE (206) 442-5504/0290 OR UNITED STATES MARSHAL SERVICE HEADQUARTERS (703) 285-1100.

A U.S. Marshal's office flier showing various "mug" shots of wanted spy Christopher Boyce

103

to sell the Russians information obtained from a friend who worked in a CIA code room. During the rest of 1975 and most of 1976, Lee regularly supplied this information. He bought a Minox camera for Boyce to photograph the documents.

One of the puzzling questions about the case is why TRW put a twenty-one-year-old college dropout in such a strategic position in the first place. At his trial, Boyce said that security at TRW was a joke, that employees drank alcohol and smoked marijuana in the black vault. Sometimes he would smuggle out classified documents in potted plants and bring them back in bags containing liquor for an employee party.[3]

In March 1976, the KGB had flown Lee to Vienna, Austria, where he gave KGB agents information about a TRW satellite that photographed the Soviet Union in an attempt to spot new missile sites. This was one of the CIA's most secret surveillance systems. The fact that the Soviets had learned about the satellite project was one reason the CIA at first hesitated to prosecute Boyce and Lee, as whatever charges levied against them would become public knowledge when revealed in the courtroom. As a CIA agent said: "If we prosecute we must . . . show . . . damage to national security, and in doing that, we often risk exposing even more information."[4]

In November 1976, at a meeting with their Soviet contacts, Boyce said he wanted to quit his job and go back to college. The KGB agents told him to study Russian and Chinese, so he could get a job in the State Department, and continue his spying activities there. Boyce did quit in December, but there was to be one more TRW delivery.

The delivery concerned information about the "Pyramider Project," which entailed sending a satellite into orbit that would always be in radio contact with CIA headquarters in Langley, Virginia, so that CIA agents could relay messages to Langley from anywhere in the world via a hand-held radio transmitter. A copy of the feasibility study for "Pyramider" was kept in the black vault, and it is assumed that Boyce gave the document to the KGB, as the photographs taken from Lee at his arrest had the word "pyramider" on them.

Of Spies and Satellites: Espionage in the 1970s

The morning before Lee's arrest, he had gone to one of his signal spots, and with adhesive tape, pasted an "x" on a lamppost. The "x" meant he had a delivery for "John," his KGB contact, who was actually Boris Grishin, who worked under the cover of a science attaché at the Soviet Embassy in Mexico City. When Grishin saw the "x," he was supposed to meet Lee at a certain restaurant at 8 P.M. Grishin never showed up. Lee then followed an alternate plan of returning to the restaurant at 10 A.M. the next day. But again Grishin did not appear. Although Lee had been warned never to go to the Soviet Embassy, he nevertheless went there to deliver his information, most likely because he needed the money he would be paid for his stolen documents.

Before their espionage venture, the two boys seemed to have everything going for them. Why did they turn against their country? Lee testified that he spied because Boyce tricked him into believing they were acting as CIA agents leaking false information to the Soviets. Lee's mother, however, blames his spying on his involvement with drugs and his obsession with making money.

Christopher Boyce claimed Lee was blackmailing him to spy. According to Boyce, he told Lee he had seen evidence that the CIA was trying to subvert Australian labor unions, who were opposed to the agency's using two Australian bases for collecting satellite photos of the USSR and other countries. The bases were built under a treaty according to which the United States would share the information gathered with Australia. Boyce said the United States was not sharing all the information, and he was going to write a letter revealing the deception. Lee volunteered to have the information made public, but in fact gave the information to the KGB. He threatened to send a copy of the letter to the FBI and TRW if Boyce did not supply more classified information for the Soviet Union.

A third theory as to why Lee and Boyce spied for the Soviets is that they had become disillusioned with the U.S. government for its involvement in the Vietnam war and the Watergate scandal. Especially disheartening was President Richard Nixon's resignation, steps away from impeachment for authorizing members of his staff, including two CIA agents, to steal files from the

Democratic party's national headquarters at the Watergate hotel complex in Washington, D.C. Boyce's parish priest confirms this theory, saying Boyce's most outstanding quality was his idealism of church and state. "Then came Watergate," the priest said, "and everything else and it was all a great disillusion to him."[5]

The prosecution's contention, however, was that Boyce and Lee were only two of countless young people in the 1960s and 1970s who were disillusioned by Vietnam and Watergate—who found ways to express their disappointment in the U.S. government other than selling national security information to the Russians and thereby jeopardizing the lives of Americans.

Lee and Boyce were found guilty of delivering and transmitting information to the USSR relating to the defense of the United States. Andrew Daulton Lee was sentenced to life in prison, and Christopher Boyce to forty years. Both were sent to Lompoc Prison in California.

On the evening of January 21, 1980, after his appeal for a reduction in sentence was turned down, Christopher Boyce left a papier-mâché model of himself lying on the cot in his cell and hid in a drainage tunnel beneath the guard tower. Then, using a makeshift ladder, Boyce scaled a ten-foot high fence, cut through the alarm system wires, leaped to the other side, and disappeared into the night. For the next nineteen months, U.S. marshals, who are responsible for apprehending federal fugitives, followed leads to Central America, Europe, and South Africa.

Finally, during an investigation of bank robberies in Washington state, FBI agents thought they recognized a disguised Boyce in bank photos taken during some of the robberies. The marshals concentrated on the Olympic Peninsula, one of the state's last reserves of peregrine falcons, Boyce's passion. In checking drivers' licenses in the area, investigators found one with a photograph that looked like Boyce, issued to an Anthony Edward Lester, in Forks, Washington.

When marshals went to the address listed on the license, they found Kaye and Jerry Sullivan living there. The Sullivans said the license photo was the same "Sean" who had taken Jerry fishing on his $65,000 boat. Kaye Sullivan said "Sean just kind of hung

Of Spies and Satellites: Espionage in the 1970s

out at our home. We didn't pry into his life."[6] FBI agents then posed as oil drillers in Forks to pick up more clues about Boyce.

One night agents overheard a conversation in a tavern, in which the bartender told a young man who had just come in that he had seen "Sean" in Port Angeles. The next day, agents staked out a twenty-five block area in Port Angeles. On August 21, 1981, agents saw Boyce sitting in a beat-up car eating a hamburger in front of a fast-food stand. Guns drawn, they surrounded him. "Drop that hamburger," one agent shouted.[7] In Boyce's car trunk, FBI agents found two wigs, false sideburns, a rifle, and money stolen from a Washington bank. Boyce had been taking flying lessons and was to receive his pilot's license in a few days, after which he planned to take flight. Now, however, the Falcon's wings were clipped. He was flying nowhere.

The theft of the KH-11 manual allowed the Soviets to block the effectiveness of a U.S. surveillance system that American officials believed would keep the United States ahead of the Russians for years. The Soviets could use the manual to make a fuse that would "blind" the satellite (make it inoperative), thereby preventing it from detecting whether the Soviet Union was abiding by a strategic arms limitation treaty.

As to who gave the KH-11 manual to the Russians first—William Kampiles or Christopher Boyce and Andrew Daulton Lee—only the CIA knows for sure.

10
Bugs, Subs, and Lasers: Modern Spy Gadgets

In 1952, U.S. Ambassador to Moscow George F. Kennan sat in his study reading out loud. There was a reason for his "talking to the walls." Somewhere in the room the KGB had hidden a bug, a secret listening device. Taking advantage of this knowledge, Kennan hoped the eavesdropping KGB would believe what he read was an authentic message to Washington. As Kennan read, electronic technicians scurried about the room with detection instruments, trying to home in on the bug. Suddenly one of the technicians snatched a wooden replica of the Great Seal of the United States from the wall and smashed it open.

"Quivering with excitement," Ambassador Kennan recalled, "the technician extracted from the shattered . . . seal a small device not much larger than a pencil. With this discovery, the whole art of intergovernmental eavesdropping was raised to a new technological level."[1]

A short time later, a Japanese electronics expert demonstrated to the National Security Agency, the U.S. intelligence organization responsible for electronic gadgetry and secret codes, how these bugs could be inserted into lamps, ashtrays, fountain pens, and other objects, in order to emit radio signals that could not be detected by counterintelligence devices then in use. Thus, the "sneaky," a secret listening device planted within an intelligence target, was officially adopted into U.S. espionage arsenals.

Within months, the gimmickry expert known by the code name "Jojo" in the CIA's Office of Special Operations (OSO), had found a wealth of espionage gadgets, invented by companies

Bugs, Subs, and Lasers: Modern Spy Gadgets

such as IBM, General Electric, and DuPont, that had been tucked away in their copyright safes because there was no immediate commercial value in manufacturing them.

Included in the treasure trove were tiny devices planted in typewriters that transmitted what was typed to a receiving center miles away; a chemically treated handkerchief which, after one minute of exposure to air, would pick up traces of factory fumes that could be analyzed to discover what products different factories were producing; and desk sponges for wetting stamps, which could pick up traces of "body chemistry" that, when analyzed, revealed descriptions of people who had been in the room during the period of exposure.

Today intelligence services also use spying gadgets for "dirty tricks." The CIA, for example, has a warehouse filled with equipment to provide assassins weapons for undetected killing. The warehouse's science rooms contain almost every poison and killing bacteria known, as well as liquids and pills containing chemicals to disorient or humiliate victims. One pill can cause victims to emit such a foul odor that no one can stand to be in the same room with them.

In 1956, when then Egyptian President Gamal Abdel Nasser nationalized the Suez Canal, Britain asked the United States for help in assassinating Nasser. The plan drawn up was to inject a deadly poison into a pack of Kent cigarettes, known to be Nasser's favorite brand. CIA agent Miles Copeland was selected to give Nasser the deadly pack, since Copeland had built up a close personal relationship with the president. In order to avoid suspicion, Copeland would smoke one of the poisoned cigarettes, too. He was given a syringe containing an antidote which he was to inject himself with within an hour after smoking the cigarette. The plan was eventually dropped. In the 1960s a similar plan was proposed then dropped that would have used poisoned Cuban cigars to assassinate Fidel Castro.

Today the bugging devices of the 1950s have shrunk to the size of a grain of rice and can be planted anywhere—in a wall, a chair, or on a person's clothing. An often-used scene in spy movies shows the hero or heroine overcoming a bugged room by talking in low voices while in the background a radio plays loud music and faucets are turned on full blast. The truth is, however, if the sounds are picked up by several bugs scattered around a room, a computer can compare the soundtracks from different angles, pick out the voice vibrations, and edit out the background noise.

Therefore, to avoid being overheard by microwave beams or other bugs in the woodwork, U.S. embassies and consulates hold important conversations in "secure rooms." These are rooms within rooms, shielded by a plastic bubble to prevent the penetration or escape of all sound and electromagnetic energy, such as radio signals or microwaves. Properly constructed and inspected, these rooms are 100 percent secure.

Sometimes, however, U.S. diplomats like Ambassador Kennan *want* the Soviets to hear what they are saying, either to feed them misinformation, or, amazingly, to demand repairs and other services from the USSR's notoriously uncooperative government service agency. In one case, a security officer's wife at the American Embassy in Moscow complained to her kitchen walls about the disappearance of her favorite butcher knife. A few days later she came home to find a lump under the living room rug. Her knife had been returned.

Outside the embassies, Soviet bugging of American apartments is so easily replaced that U.S. officials do not bother "sweeping" their rooms for bugs. Instead, they often employ toy "magic slates" for saying things they do not want overheard. Today the KGB can monitor phone conversations even when the receiver is on the hook. As a result, many Russians disconnect their telephones or bury them in pillows when friends visit. And the KGB's use of directional microphones makes it impossible to carry on a safe conversation even outdoors.

Bugs hidden in electric typewriters or printers can pick up and transmit electronic signals given off by each key or by the ball in a Selectric-style typewriter. People receiving the transmissions outside the building can read the message almost as easily as if they were looking over the typist's shoulder.

Especially hard to detect are bugs that do not transmit through the air. Instead, they are attached by wires to listening posts outside a building. The connecting wires can be anything that conducts electricity, such as an air-conditioning vent or metallic paint under the surface paint of a room. Finding these bugs involves X-raying every square inch of a building or tearing apart the walls.

Some eavesdropping methods have been created that use no bugs at all. One such method was created when some farsighted technicians realized the microwave oven could be turned into a spy gadget. Microwave beams, the short radio waves used in microwave ovens, are now used to listen in on radar messages and long-distance telephone calls.

Microwave bugging works by radiation pulses being aimed at a target by radar-type dishes hidden somewhere nearby. Then resonators—instruments or surfaces that vibrate in response to pressure changes produced in the air by the spoken word—are picked up by the microwave beam as it reflects off them. The resonator vibrations are transmitted back to a receiver. There, they are treated electronically to reproduce the conversation, in a way similar to how a record reproduces music.

Computers are another bugless source of eavesdropping. Computers give off radio waves that can be picked up by interception equipment outside a building and then translated by another computer. In fact, intelligence experts say computers are the most insecure places to store information. According to a 1985 Department of Defense (DOD) study on computer security, only 30 out of every 17,000 DOD computers are even minimally safe against hackers.[2]

The latest state of the art in eavesdropping is the laser beam. Since sounds and words cause windows and other surfaces to vibrate, a laser beam is directed at a window or any surface that vibrates with sound waves. The beam is reflected and picks up the vibrations from the window. A computer then reads the beam and converts it back into sound.

Today it is possible for a building itself to become a bug. Cavities incorporated into prefabricated structures conduct sounds to points outside the building. The steel structural elements of

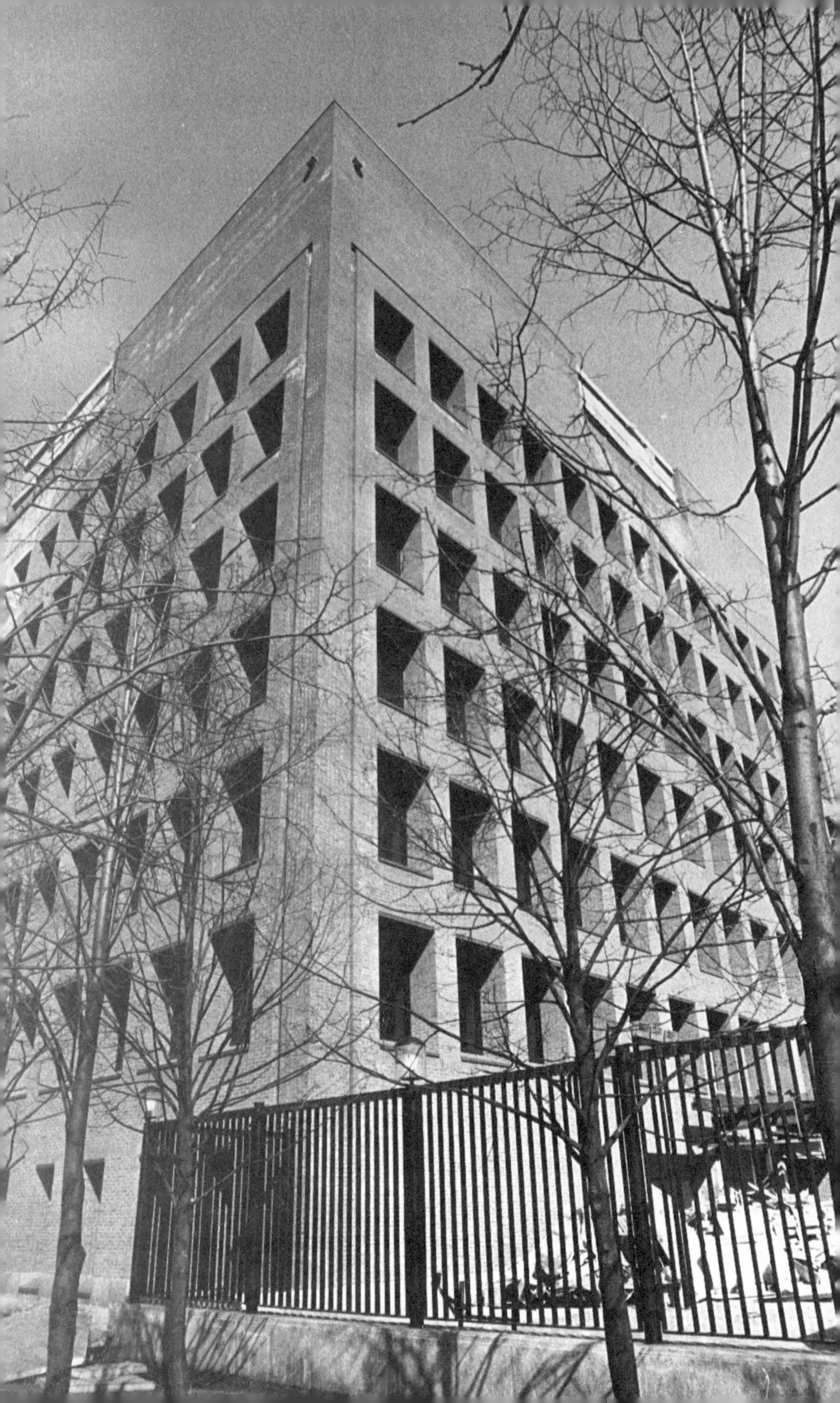

Bugs, Subs, and Lasers: Modern Spy Gadgets

the building function as a huge radio antenna to broadcast the information. In the spring of 1987, it was discovered that this was how the Russians had turned the new American Embassy in Moscow, under construction since 1977, into a bug. According to Congressman Dick Armey (Republican-Texas), "It's nothing but an eight-story microphone plugged into the Politburo."[3]

The Soviets were able to succeed in bugging the new American Embassy because the building was constructed from prefabricated concrete sections manufactured in Soviet factories out of sight of U.S. inspectors. Former Defense Secretary James R. Schlesinger issued a report stating that the new embassy will have to be restructured, at a cost of many tens of millions of dollars and a minimum of three years. President Reagan declared that the Soviets would not be allowed to move into their new embassy in Washington, D.C., until the new American Embassy in Moscow is secure from bugging devices.

Information picked up by bugging devices is often sent to the intelligence agency's headquarters by clandestine radio messages. The radio frequencies used are difficult to detect and even harder to decipher, since espionage reports are transmitted in language that sounds like ordinary messages used by commercial businesses.

Secret communications equipment can be installed in a simple battery-operated, transistor radio. The old spy movies are outdated that showed security agents bursting in on someone wearing large earphones, while hunched over a wireless sending a secret message to the USSR. Gone too are the huge transmission sets with aerial wires running out the window, such as the one Soviet spy Rudolf Abel used. Today U.S. security agents might burst into a room to find the spy propped in an easy chair, listening to "music" on his "transistor."

A variation of the secret radio message is the "screech," a tape-recorded message speeded up so that it sounds like a high-pitched whine. The "screech" is played in the background while the sender gives a harmless "ham" radio message. A tape recorder at the other end records the screech, then plays it back at a slower speed, so the "hidden" message can be heard.

A 1987 view of the U.S. Embassy in Moscow,
scene of many bugging allegations

Another way of sending stolen secrets is by microdots, which can reduce documents to a size small enough to be hidden in ordinary objects that can be sent through the mail. To imagine how small a microdot is, the dot on the "i" in the word "microdot" can conceal a page of text the size of this page. The drawback is that microdots can be spotted by anyone who is told what to look for.

At first, microdots were frequently hidden in secret compartments of suitcases. However, the worldwide crackdown by customs officials on heroin smuggling has virtually made the secret compartment useless. Instead, chemically treated notepads for writing with invisible ink are often used. The spy writes a nonincriminating cover message, then writes the espionage report in colorless ink between the lines, and mails the letter in an ordinary mailbox.

In today's space-age world, satellites have joined the warehouses of techno-spying. Flying in high orbit, these satellites, called "Spies in the Sky," can identify different makes of automobiles, read license plates, and distinguish between a Guernsey or a Hereford cow in a field.

There are two forms of electronic gadgetry intelligence—imaging and signals. Imaging involves photographs obtained by cameras attached to satellites or aircraft, which are used to observe military and industrial installations and to monitor arms control compliance. One satellite turn around the world can tell the status of all such installations within its range. Over a period of years, photographic analysts can look at changes in these photographs to judge how far a country's military capability has progressed.

The most advanced photo satellite is the KH-11, the plans for which were presumably given to the Soviets by either William Kampiles or Andrew Lee and Christopher Boyce. The KH-11, instead of using film, converts its pictures into digital radio impulses and immediately relays them to a ground station.

Signals intelligence (SIGINT), the second type of electronic spying, involves the interception of coded or uncoded diplomatic or military communications, called COMINT. In the United

Bugs, Subs, and Lasers: Modern Spy Gadgets

States, COMINT is processed by four acres of computers at the National Security Agency in Washington. The computers scan intercepted cables and telephone calls at high speed, selecting which ones to print out by key words programmed into the computers. SIGINT is collected using satellites, aircraft, and submarines. One of the United States' most advanced spy planes is the high-altitude SR-71 which, flying at 85,000 feet and traveling at more than 2,000 miles per hour, can film 60,000 square miles in an hour.

To provide early warning against a nuclear attack, SIGINT satellites detect signals in microwave pulses given off by air defense radar, either on a ship or by the flash of a nuclear detonation. The United States also uses specially equipped satellites to pick up radio messages and to map radar installations. Radar installations, placed literally on the USSR's doorstep, have kept the United States abreast of the Soviet Union's progress in developing ballistic missiles. SIGINT also includes missile telemetry, by which a missile or warhead sends back to earth data on its performance.

In America, the most important SIGINT satellite is codenamed Rhyolite. In his book, *The Falcon and the Snowman*, author Robert Lindsey says a Rhyolite can "monitor Communist microwave radio and long-distance telephone traffic over much of the Eurasian landmass, eavesdropping on a Soviet commissar in Moscow talking to his mistress in Yalta or on a general talking to his subordinate on another continent."[4]

Besides satellites and spy planes, the third way of gathering electronic intelligence is by submarine. Both the United States and the Soviet Union give high priority to tracking each other's subs and to keeping their own hidden. This cat-and-mouse spy game involves high stakes, since as many nuclear warheads are deployed by submarines as are deployed by land silos and bombers combined.

The U.S. Navy tracks Soviet subs by means of a network of sophisticated listening devices, called hydrophones. This sound surveillance system (SOSUS) consists of placing the hydrophones on the ocean bottom at strategic points that Soviet subs would have to cross to get into position for a nuclear strike. The hydrophones collect ocean sounds hundreds of miles away and transmit them, via cable, to onshore computer centers. There, supercomputers sift through the noises for the telltale "signatures" of Russian subs, which often can provide even the name of the Soviet vessel and its hull number.

Although the Soviet Union has fast caught up with the United States in satellite and submarine technology, Soviet scientists have not kept up with U.S. development of microchips and laser beams, the staples of modern warfare. In fact the microchips produced at the high-tech firms located in Silicon Valley, south of San Francisco, California, are as valuable to the Soviets as NATO war plans. Because the ability to process masses of information in milliseconds is what makes modern weapons so deadly, the Soviet Union is waging a massive campaign to steal America's computer technology. In the 1970s, for instance, while touring a U.S. aircraft factory, Soviet engineers went so far as to wear sticky-soled shoes to pick up metal filings.

The Soviets decide what to steal by reading American technical journals. A favorite is *Aviation Week and Space Technology*, which prints so much informative scientific material that it has been nicknamed "Aviation Leak." Soviet officials make up shopping lists for electronic gadgets to be stolen, and KGB agents are required to produce at least four items a year from the list.

Because practically any high-tech item can be turned into a military weapon, new U.S. export laws ban the sale of more than 200,000 such products. The microcircuitry of some video games, for instance, can be reengineered into guided missiles. One example is Texas Instruments' "Speak & Spell" game, which until recently was under export controls because it contained an embedded microprocessor. "The Russians are sweating," says Customs Service Commissioner William von Raab. "They used to be able to carry off all our technology by the truckload. Now we're making them pay more and take longer."[5]

To counteract these strict export laws, the KGB has created dummy corporations in Europe to buy high-tech exports from Western techno-bandits, who are eager to collect the Soviets' 500 percent markups by acting as middlemen. In fact, there are so many techno-bandits around that the KGB auctions off almost every sale.

Without proper safeguards, the day may come when Soviet intelligence can plug into Defense Department computers that control American nuclear weapons. Then the fictional movie *War Games* will become a devastating reality. If, as government posters warned during World War II, "Loose lips sink ships," then loose microchips could launch missiles in the next.

11

A Family Affair: The John Walker Spy Ring

Around noon on May 19, 1985, John A. Walker, Jr., forty-seven, a former Navy communications expert, drove his van into the Washington, D.C., suburbs. On the way, he circled around and around blocks, made U-turns, and frequently pulled to the side of the road and looked behind him, as if he were being pursued. Finally he stopped on a country road outside the rural town of Poolesville, Maryland, where he placed a brown paper bag under a tree and dropped a crumpled soda can on the ground. Then he drove around the area for three hours, glancing out of the van every time he passed the brown paper bag.

That evening, John Walker checked into a Maryland motel. As he walked down the hall outside his room, FBI agents surrounded him. John tried to fend them off and in the scuffle dropped a long white envelope on the floor. Inside was a map showing secret drop points in the Washington area and instructions on how to avoid surveillance at drop sites. The instructions were written by Aleksey Tkachenko, a Soviet diplomat, KGB agent, and John Walker's Russian contact in the United States. Within days, newspapers headlined the story that John Walker was the leader of a Soviet spy ring that for nearly eighteen years had been stealing U.S. naval secrets for the Russians.

Three days after John Walker's arrest for espionage, his son Michael, twenty-two, a Navy yeoman 3/c, was arrested as an accomplice. A month later, two more members of the spy ring were arrested. One was John's brother, Arthur, fifty, a Navy veteran specializing in submarine warfare, who worked in main-

A Family Affair: The John Walker Spy Ring

tenance of amphibious vessels at a Navy defense contracting firm in Alexandria, Virginia. The other was John Walker's best friend, Jerry Whitworth, forty-five, an unemployed, retired Navy communications specialist and satellite expert who had served at a highly secret Navy base in the Indian Ocean.

The Walker espionage ring first began to unravel in November, 1984, when John's wife, Barbara, went to the FBI and informed on him. She said John had been recruited by the Soviets in 1968, when he was a Navy petty officer. Barbara claimed that she had started to notice odd behavior in John around 1970. He would travel to Washington and leave paper bags filled with what she later learned was classified material under a tree. On one trip, he returned with $35,000. John's odd behavior induced Barbara to pry open his desk, where she found instructions telling John where to make his next deliveries.

Barbara claimed John's motive for spying was pure greed. He needed money to save a failing restaurant business, and he "loved the glamour of being a spy. He loved walking down the street and knowing something no one else . . . knew."[1] For thirteen years, Barbara tormented herself about whether to go to the FBI. During this time, she and John divorced, and John retired from the Navy, eventually opening three private investigation agencies in Norfolk, Virginia, where he continued to spy for the Soviets. As a private eye, John searched other people's offices for bugs, while at the same time planting bugs in defense contractors' offices. And, as a retired Navy officer, he could get on any Navy, Marine, or Air Force base, where he would steal important papers.

After Barbara's tip-off, the FBI wiretapped John's phones. For almost six months, federal investigators heard nothing incriminating enough to arrest him. Then on May 19, 1985, FBI agents overheard John talking to someone about a planned trip to Charlotte, North Carolina. But instead of heading for North Carolina, agents followed him to Maryland, observed him drop the brown paper bag and the soda can at the side of a road, and thus found the incriminating evidence they needed.

Although Aleksey Tkachenko, John's Soviet contact, had been

seen driving around the Maryland countryside that same night, he never picked up the brown bag, as that afternoon an FBI agent had unwittingly picked up the crumpled soda can, which was the signal that John had not been followed. Tkachenko left the United States five days later.

Inside the paper bag were 129 classified Navy documents from the aircraft carrier *Nimitz* and a letter describing the activities of code-named Navy associates, such as "S" and "D." A search of John's home turned up letters revealing the identities of these associates. One letter was from Michael Walker, mailed from his post aboard the *Nimitz*, revealing him to be "S." Navy investigators later found fifteen pounds of classified material in Michael's bunk area. Another letter showed that "K" was Arthur Walker. Unauthorized documents about new amphibious ships, including two designed to serve as command centers during a sea-launched invasion of the United States, were found in Arthur's office.

A third letter was written by John Walker to his Soviet contact about one member of the ring who had quit. John wrote that the quitter's expensive lifestyle would bring him back into espionage within two years, as he would not be able to adjust to living off his wife's income, would probably fail as a stockbroker, and earn only a modest living in computer sales. Letters written by Jerry Whitworth to John about becoming a stockbroker and entering computer sales were later recovered.

In putting the evidence together, the FBI realized that Jerry Whitworth was the unknown person who had written three anonymous letters to the FBI in 1984. The first two told about an espionage ring that for twenty years had been giving Soviet agents cryptographic key lists for military communications. The third anonymous letter, however, dated August 13, 1984, said the sender had changed his mind about exposing the spy ring.

According to John's friends, he had never given any hint of his Communist connections, but instead presented himself as a vehement anti-Communist. One of his friends told the FBI that John once became enraged over a news story about a convicted Soviet spy who John thought had been given too light a sentence.

John Walker, left, is led out of a Maryland detention center in 1985.

While John Walker imagined himself to be another James Bond, Michael Walker and Jerry Whitworth were the complete opposites of the fictional super spy. Michael, a surfer, loved partying. His friends were shocked when he joined the Navy, claiming such a serious move did not fit his carefree personality. Jerry Whitworth's neighbors called him an "all-American man." He was active in civic work in his community, including a neighborhood anticrime program.

All four men had worked in communications in the Navy's most sensitive area—undersea nuclear forces. Out of the U.S. triad of nuclear defense areas, consisting of B-52 bombers, land-based ballistic missiles, and submarine forces, the submarines are considered the most valuable. Hidden deep under the ocean, armed with multiwarhead missiles, and always changing positions, the fleet of Poseidon and Trident submarines could by themselves destroy the Soviet Union many times over.

While working for the Navy, John and Arthur Walker had information both on how the United States locates Soviet subs and operates its subs silently, making them harder to detect. Because the exact information that the Walker spy ring gave the Soviets is unknown, we may never know the extent of the damage caused by them, as publishing details about the information they gave the Soviet Union could give the Russians facts they might not already know. How much information to make public is an ongoing dilemma in prosecuting and convicting spies.

The most damaging information stolen was probably reports on malfunctions of antisubmarine-warfare equipment, since explaining what did not work requires explaining how the equipment does operate. In addition, both John Walker and Jerry Whitworth had been cryptographers on ships engaged in spotting submarines. According to an electronics expert, cryptographers "are the keepers of the kingdom. All the information in an organization ultimately goes through their hands."[2] Therefore, if the Soviets were given the codes and radio frequencies used by U.S. sub trackers, the Russians could intercept information about U.S. tracking capabilities merely by listening in.

One piece of information intelligence experts believe the Soviets obtained from the Walker ring was the importance of, and the knowledge how, to build quiet submarines to make detection harder. Soviet subs had been extremely noisy until the 1970s, when the Walker ring got under way.

A Family Affair: The John Walker Spy Ring

The Navy has said it will take $100 million to repair the damage caused by the Walker spy ring. Some of the repairs include reducing by 10 percent the 900,000 Navy personnel cleared for handling classified information, starting random lie-detector tests of naval personnel to detect spying, and cutting 10 percent of the 4 million people given security clearances in all U.S. military branches.

After his indictment, John Walker turned state's evidence and testified against Jerry Whitworth, his best friend, in return for a lighter sentence for Michael. John claimed Whitworth had stolen copies of communications plans in the event of hostilities in the Middle East. On August 28, 1986, Jerry Whitworth was found guilty not only of espionage but of income tax evasion as well, for failing to report $332,000 he received from spying. He was sentenced to 365 years in prison and fined $410,000. By levying that great a fine, the judge made sure that any money Whitworth might earn, either in prison or by selling the book or movie rights to his life story, would go to the government. Jerry Whitworth will be eligible for parole at age 107, if he lives that long.

At the time of sentencing, the Justice Department released a statement by Soviet defector Vitali Yurchenko, who had defected to the United States in July 1985, only to redefect to the Soviet Union four months later, claiming he had been drugged and kidnapped by the CIA. Yurchenko's statement said the Soviets believed the Walker spy operation was the most important in the KGB's history, and that secrets supplied by the ring allowed the Soviets to decode more than 1 million U.S. military messages.

Arthur Walker was sentenced to three life terms, plus forty years in prison, and Michael Walker to twenty-five years. Both John and Michael had made a plea-bargain in which they pledged to cooperate with attempts to assess the national security damage done by the ring, provided they received the sentences the judge imposed.

On November 6, 1986, a federal judge, expressing "utter contempt and disgust" for John Walker, sentenced him to life in prison and vowed to "do everything in my power" to prevent him from ever being paroled. The judge noted that John Walker's motive was pure greed, as he had been paid approximately $1 million for his spying and had recruited members of his family into the network to obtain even more money.[3] John had tried to get his daughter Laura to join the spy ring in 1979, but she refused. At the time, Laura was an Army communications operator, which would have given the ring entry into the U.S. Army as well as the Navy. Laura testified that in order to convince her to join the ring, John told her she would never amount to anything anyway, and if she spied she would never have to worry about having enough money.

In the United States, the year 1985 could have been called "the year of the spy," as eleven major espionage operations were uncovered that year. One was that of Richard Miller, forty-nine, the first FBI agent ever to be charged with espionage. Miller was arrested for passing FBI secrets to Svetlana Ogorodnikova, a Russian emigré, and Nikolai Wolfson, her estranged husband, in return for $50,000 in gold and $15,000 in cash.

Three more espionage operations were exposed within one week of each other at the end of November. All three pointed to lapses in U.S. security procedures, although they were the result of a recent crackdown on security measures by U.S. intelligence agencies. As one intelligence official said: "The bad news is that the spying was going on. The good news is that we caught them."[4]

One of the spies arrested was Ronald William Pelton, forty-four, a former communications specialist for the National Security Agency. Pelton was charged with selling electronics surveillance secrets to the KGB, which might have given the Soviets the means of intercepting coded American satellite communications, and thereby the means to render ineffective some of the most sophisticated U.S. intelligence devices used for monitoring Soviet communications. Pelton was sentenced to life in prison.

Another intelligence blow for the United States occurred when fired CIA agent Edward Lee Howard defected to the Soviet Union, taking with him the names of Russian CIA agents in Moscow. Then on November 23, naturalized American Larry Wu-tai Chin, sixty-three, a CIA agent since 1952, became the first U.S. citizen

A Family Affair: The John Walker Spy Ring

ever arrested for spying for the People's Republic of China. Larry Chin, who gave China virtually every top secret U.S. document on the Far East since the 1970s, committed suicide in his jail cell.

Two days before Chin's arrest, American Jonathan J. Pollard, thirty-one, was caught as he raced across Washington, D.C., toward the Israeli Embassy to ask for asylum. Pollard was charged with selling Navy secrets to Israel while working in a Navy counterterrorism unit that focused on the Middle East. The documents he stole included satellite photos, data on Soviet weaponry, and locations of U.S. ships and training exercises. A major concern of U.S. officials was that Israel's intelligence agencies might have been penetrated by Soviet agents, and thus the material Pollard stole could fall into their hands.

Pollard pleaded guilty, saying he spied to help Israel and meant no harm to the United States. He was sentenced to life in prison. His wife, charged with delivering U.S. defense secrets to the Israelis, was sentenced to five years in prison.

Israeli Prime Minister Yitzhak Shamir apologized for what he called an unauthorized, "rogue" espionage operation. He claimed the Israeli Defense Ministry's intelligence agency, Lekem, which recruited Pollard, had been disbanded, and promised that the Shin Bet, Israel's FBI, would conduct an investigation into the case. Ex-Foreign Minister Abba Eban announced that a Knesset (Israel's Parliament) intelligence subcommittee would also make an inquiry into the case.

In America, Jewish organizations expressed outrage at Pollard's spying. Abraham H. Foxman, associate national director of the Anti-Defamation League, said: "What we reject is the inference that support of Israel legitimizes criminal action against the United States."[5] In Los Angeles, a Jewish newspaper, the *B'nai B'rith Messenger*, published an editorial saying, "For the first time Israel has involved us in an unworthy incident," and the Israeli government should give assurances that "this can never happen again."[6]

The exposure especially strained relations between Israel and the United States when Israel promoted two key men in the case,

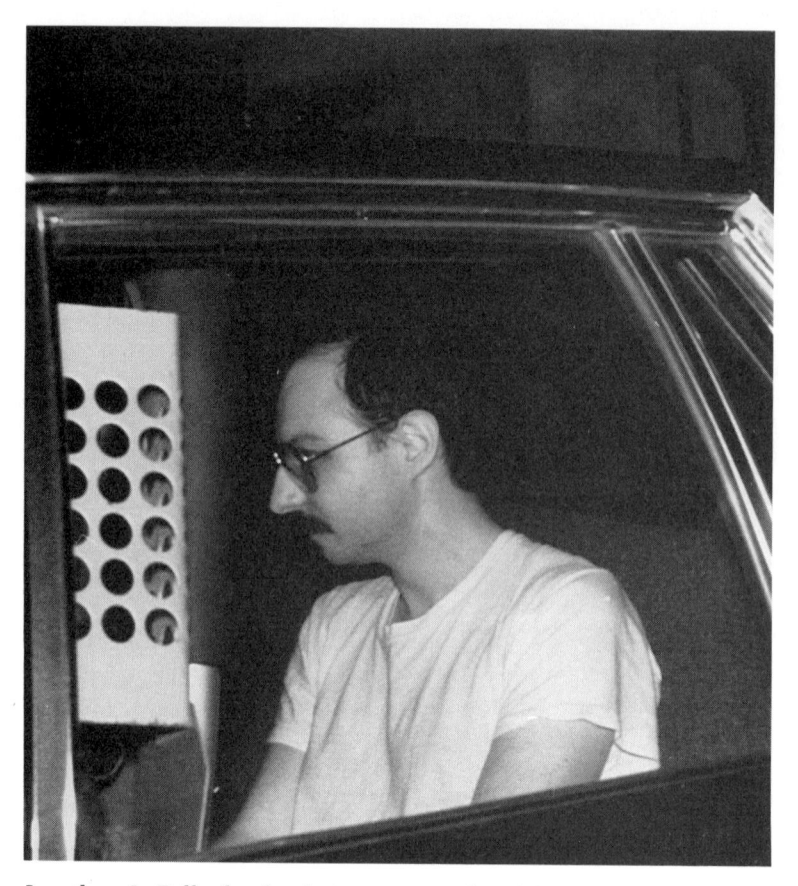

Jonathan J. Pollard, after being sentenced to life in prison for selling Israel many secret U.S. military documents

instead of reprimanding them. One was Rafael Eitan, reportedly the leader of the Lekem operation, who was named chairman of the board of Israel Chemicals Company, the country's largest government-owned corporation. The other Israeli, Colonel Aviem Sella, who first handled Pollard's espionage activities in 1984, was given command of Tel Nof airbase, one of Israel's most strategic military facilities.

On March 3, 1987, a U.S. federal grand jury indicted Sella on charges of espionage, the first official of an American ally ever charged with spying against the United States. Sella cannot be

A Family Affair: The John Walker Spy Ring

extradited, however, as the U.S.-Israeli extradition treaty does not name espionage as a reason for extradition. After two years of angry protests by the United States, Sella resigned his command in April 1987, and Prime Minister Shamir appointed an independent investigative committee to study the case and make recommendations.

This panel concluded that the Israeli government as a whole should assume responsibility for the Pollard affair, and that no senior officials knew about the case until after Pollard's arrest. The Israeli cabinet voted to accept the panel's recommendations. The Knesset's intelligence subcommittee, however, while reaching the same conclusions as the government-appointed panel, nevertheless focused blame on former Prime Minister Shimon Peres, current Prime Minister Yitzhak Shamir, Defense Minister Yitzhak Rabin, and former Defense Minister Moshe Arens, because the Lekem was under their supervision, and therefore should have been supervised more closely.

The Pollard case did not end there. In August 1987, Rafael Eitan, leader of the Pollard spy operation, announced that he had acted with approval from his superiors, in effect contradicting the other two committees' conclusions that no senior officials knew about the case. Those committees are now demanding that Defense Minister Rabin issue a clarification about who approved Eitan's actions.

*   *   *

What does the future hold for intelligence agencies? Do they have too much power?

The CIA has been criticized continually for having either too much or too little power. Just as the CIA's abuses of power and spying on U.S. citizens in the 1970s pushed the pendulum toward decreasing the number of CIA agent-oriented operations in favor of using more electronic eavesdropping, so in the 1980s, the exposure of espionage cases such as Ronald Pelton's and the Walkers', in which U.S. electronic spying secrets were sold to the Soviets, have pushed the CIA power pendulum toward the side of more human spying. For if human spies are caught, they can tell the other side only what they know. But if the mechanics of a spy satellite are found out, the other side knows exactly what the satellite was looking at and how it was looking at it.

Moreover, only human beings can learn what weapons are being built inside factories, obtain blueprints of these weapons systems and war-planning documents, and then evaluate the information collected so that government leaders can make vital decisions regarding military needs and foreign policy. With nuclear weapons available on both sides of the Iron Curtain, however, today's intelligence agencies are more interested in discovering what the enemy's *intentions* are rather than how many weapons the opposition has. As a former CIA official said, "The President is not so much interested in the number of warheads on a missile as he is in what the Soviets might do with these weapons."[7]

Another area of concern for intelligence agencies today is the increased number of people handling classified documents, which increases the number of people who could become spies for an "enemy" government. In the United States, for example, there are approximately 4 million American civilians and 121 Soviet emigrés holding security clearances, most of whom work for the CIA and other defense-related industries.

Recent KGB successes in the United States point to the failure of American intelligence agencies to check thoroughly all their employees for security clearances, and to heed warning signs that some of their employees might be vulnerable to Soviet recruitment. For example, a thorough security check of John Walker would have revealed that his low financial status versus his desire to own luxuries made him a prime target for Soviet recruitment.

Convicted "Falcon" spy Christopher Boyce reported that security measures were so lax at TRW that employees got away with growing marijuana plants in the black vault and using the code-destruction blender there to mix banana daiquiris. In addition, while his sister had to take a polygraph test to get a job at a 7-Eleven store, investigators looking into Boyce's own security clearance took no notice of his counterculture life style before letting him handle top secret documents.

A Family Affair: The John Walker Spy Ring

Commenting on the ease with which people obtain security clearances in the United States, Delaware Senator William Roth said, "It's harder to get an American Express Card."[8] And, although in the United States reclearance checks are required every five years, due to a ten-year backlog of checks this procedure is not always followed. During the fifteen years that Jerry Whitworth spied for Russia, for instance, he was recleared only twice. To help reduce the chances for another Walker-type spy operation, American intelligence agencies are attempting first to reduce the number of jobs requiring security clearances and then to overhaul the procedures for the issuance of these security clearances.

Is there anything to be learned from spy operations exposed in the past in order to prevent, or at least lessen, the possibility of citizens committing treason against their countries? Is there any reason to believe that spying will one day disappear?

James B. Stockell, a retired Navy vice-admiral who spent seven years as a prisoner of war in Vietnam, comments on the reason people betray their countries today, saying, "The missing element is a clear sense of what is right and wrong, and the resolve . . . to live according to that sense."[9]

Other experts who have studied traitors such as FBI agent Richard Miller and National Security Agency employee Ronald Pelton claim these people have no sense of national loyalty—of being a part of a country and thereby responsible for that country's fate and honor. Also accounting for the prevalence of people who spy against their countries today is the fact that these people are a different breed than the Rosenbergs, Philbys, and Lonsdales of the 1950s, who may have betrayed their countries for ideological reasons. Today's spies sell out primarily for money but also for the imagined romance and excitement involved. These motives have won out over the concept of national loyalty and honor.

As a result of this lack of national loyalty, all intelligence organizations remain vulnerable to penetration. In spite of each agency's successes in breaking up spy operations against their countries, there is always the frustrating reality that tomorrow's headlines could just as easily bring news of a completely new spy operation. Further, the inherent secretive nature of intelligence organizations makes it difficult to assess their effectiveness, as only their espionage failures receive publicity.

Thus it seems that even with stricter security measures, better trained intelligence agents, and the most sophisticated electronic espionage devices possible, it is likely that no country will ever entirely eliminate the penetration of its intelligence secrets by enemy agents. For as long as there are people who believe that betraying their country is permissible, whether for ideological reasons, financial gain, or paying off a blackmailer, then there will always be "spies among us."

Notes

Chapter 1

1. *The Los Angeles Times*, 15 July 1986, 1.
2. P. Knightley, *The Second Oldest Profession* (New York: Norton, 1986), 318.
3. *Time*, 27 July 1987, 9.
4. *The Los Angeles Times*, 5 August 1987, 17.
5. *Ibid.*
6. *The Los Angeles Times*, 25 July 1987, 1.
7. *Insight*, 4 May 1987, 9.
8. J. Joesten, *They Call it Intelligence* (New York: Abelard-Schuman, 1963), 8.

Chapter 2

1. S. de Gramont, *The Secret War* (New York: Putnam, 1962), 51.
2. M. Copeland, *Without Cloak or Dagger* (Simon & Schuster, 1974), 36.
3. Gramont, *The Secret War*, 58.
4. A. Dulles, *The Craft of Intelligence* (New York: Harper & Row, 1963), 42.
5. Gramont, *The Secret War*, 20.
6. *Ibid.*
7. *Ibid.*
8. *Insight*, 23 June 1986, 6, 10.
9. *Ibid.*, 11.
10. *Ibid.*, 6.
11. Dulles, *The Craft of Intelligence*, 6.

Chapter 3

1. Dulles, *The Craft of Intelligence*, 96.
2. *U.S. News & World Report*, 15 September 1986, 28.

Chapter 4

1. Gramont, *The Secret War*, 55.
2. *Ibid.*, 56.
3. *The Washington Post Magazine*, 12 October 1986, 25.
4. *Ibid.*, 28.

Notes

5. *The Secret War*, 164.
6. *Look*, 29 October 1957, 90.
7. *Ibid.*, 91.

Chapter 5

1. *Time*, 16 April 1953, 22.
2. *Look*, 29 October 1957, 90.
3. *Time*, 29 June 1953, 8.
4. *Look*, 29 October 1957, 90.
5. *The Nation*, 15 November 1965, 365.
6. *Ibid.*, 365.
7. *Look*, 29 October 1957, 90.
8. *The Nation*, 12 September 1966, 203.
9. Gramont, *The Secret War*, 61.
10. *Ibid.*, 61.
11. *Esquire*, May 1975, 124.
12. *Ibid.*, 124.
13. *Ibid.*

Chapter 6

1. Gramont, *The Secret War*, 287.
2. *Ibid.*, 319.
3. There are conflicting sources for the names Conon Molody, Elizabeth Gee, and the Polish secret service, Z–11. The names Conon Molody and Elizabeth Gee are used in the books *The Second Oldest Profession*, *The Secret War*, and *The Craft of Intelligence*, as well as in an article printed in *U.S. News & World Report*, March 27, 1961, p. 60. The names Konon Trofimovich Molodi and Ethel Gee are used in the book *Spycatcher*, as well as in articles printed in *Newsweek*, Jan. 23, 1961, p. 22, *Newsweek*, May 1, 1964, p. 40, and *Time*, May 1, 1964, p. 33. The term Z–11 is used in *The Secret War*. The term UB is used in the book *Spycatcher*.
4. *Newsweek*, 22 March 1965, 24.
5. *U.S. News & World Report*, 23 September 1968, 11.
6. *Ibid.*, 11.
7. *Time*, 10 January 1969, 19.
8. *Ibid.*, 57.

Chapter 7

1. Joesten, *They Call it Intelligence*, 226.
2. Gramont, *The Secret War*, 391.
3. Knightley, *The Second Oldest Profession*, 299.
4. *Saturday Evening Post*, 15 February 1964, 33.
5. *Time*, 10 August 1987, 51.
6. *Saturday Evening Post*, 15 February 1964, 33.

Notes

Chapter 8

1. Gramont, *The Secret War*, 243.
2. *Newsweek*, 19 February 1962, 20.
3. Joesten, *They Call it Intelligence*, 64.
4. Dulles, *The Craft of Intelligence*, 119.
5. Gramont, *The Secret War*, 263.
6. *Ibid.*, 266.
7. Joesten, *They Call it Intelligence*, 67.
8. Gramont, *The Secret War*, 229.
9. *Ibid.*, 221.

Chapter 9

1. *Reader's Digest*, June 1979, 71.
2. *Newsweek*, 18 April 1977, 29.
3. *The Los Angeles Times*, 22 May 1979, 92.
4. *Newsweek*, 18 April 1977, 29.
5. *The Los Angeles Times*, 22 May 1977, 1.
6. *Newsweek*, 7 September 1981, 24.
7. *Ibid.*

Chapter 10

1. *The Los Angeles Times*, 13 April 1987, 1.
2. *Time*, 17 June 1985, 27.
3. *Time*, 20 April 1987, 16.
4. *Insight*, 23 June 1986, 11.
5. *Insight*, 17 June 1985, 27.

Chapter 11

1. *The Los Angeles Times*, 6 June 1985, 9.
2. *Time*, 17 June 1985, 19.
3. *The Los Angeles Times*, 7 November 1986, 6.
4. *Newsweek*, 9 December 1985, 24.
5. *The Los Angeles Times*, 18 March 1987, 8.
6. *Ibid.*
7. *Insight*, 23 June 1986, 8.
8. *Time*, 17 June 1985, 27.
9. *Ibid.*

Glossary of Spy Terms

Alternate means: other methods of gathering intelligence besides spying, from such sources as newspapers, scientific or military journals, or reports from foreign ambassadors and military attachés.

Brush exchange: a quick contact between two spies, in which classified information or messages is exchanged or delivered. Brush exchanges occur in such crowded places as football stadiums and subway stations. Ways to accomplish brush contacts are swapping shopping carts in a supermarket, swapping identical briefcases in subway stations, or letting one agent "pickpocket" another.

Case officer: supervised by the station chief, works in the target country, and is responsible for keeping complete reports about espionage operations in that country.

Counterespionage: a defensive measure to keep "enemy" agents from penetrating an intelligence operation or organization and stealing classified information.

Cover: spies' public occupations, used to "cover up" their true occupation as spies.

Cutout: a courier who passes messages between the agent and the agent's case officer or station chief.

Double agent: a spy who pretends to be working for one country's intelligence agency, but who is in reality working for another country's intelligence agency.

Drawing boards: a country's plans for future scientific or military projects.

Drop: a prearranged place for leaving messages and/or stolen classified information, for example, behind the mirror in the restroom of a restaurant.

Espionage: spying as a means of gathering intelligence.

Headquarters desk officer: furnishes the station chief with all information needed to run a particular operation. Most espionage agents work as

Glossary of Spy Terms

desk officers at the beginning of their careers, as preparation for taking over the station chief's job when his or her tour of duty ends.

Intelligence: information; in the world of spies, secret information, gathered for political, scientific, or military purposes.

Letting one's hair down: an offer, usually financial, made to a potential defector in return for his or her defection.

Microdot: secret message system in which long messages are reduced in size by a photographic process to the size of a pinhead. When the receiving agents obtain the microdot, they enlarge the message back to normal size.

Misinformation: false or misleading information, deliberately fed to "enemy" spies or governments.

Operations: the means used to gather this intelligence.

Requirements: the pieces of information (intelligence) an intelligence agency tries to acquire.

Resident: serves as the link between the case officer and espionage operations; usually a native of the country whose intelligence service employs him or her, but lives in a country next to the target country. For instance, if the target country is Syria, the resident might live in Lebanon. The resident works under the cover of a respectable citizen of the community, keeping no records or espionage equipment, and rarely, if ever, going into the target country.

Safe house: property owned by a country abroad, used by spies "on the run" as hideouts.

Special operations: covert, or secret, activities, such as handling defectors, planning assassinations, kidnappings, or getting emigré groups to operate a clandestine activity in their country.

Spitting blood: a term used to describe an agent who is hiding out because counterespionage agents have exposed his/her cover.

Station: every embassy throughout the world.

Station chief: supervises personnel who work undercover as embassy employees; controls operations run from embassy.

Surfaced: made known to the public, as when news of a defector is given to the press.

Switched off: removed from an operation, as when a spy is under surveillance by counterespionage agents, and therefore, to avoid exposure, the spy is "switched off."

Glossary of Spy Terms

Target: anything containing secret information, from an entire country to a military installation, to a filing cabinet in an office.

Third world operations: secret political operations taken by intelligence agencies in third world countries, such as sponsoring military coups or assisting a political candidate, to insure that the people running those countries are ones who favor the political policies of the intelligence agency's government.

Turned: a spy who defects is said to have "turned."

Utility operative: acquires nonclassified information required in the planning of an operation; employed by the case officer or resident to perform all the jobs that the resident, case officer, or station chief cannot do without drawing unwanted attention to themselves.

Walk-in: people who "walk in" to a foreign intelligence agency or foreign embassy to offer to spy for that agency, and/or give them classified information from their own intelligence agency or government.

Further Reading

Agee, Philip, *Inside the Company: The C.I.A. Diary*: Harmondsworth, Middlesex; England, Penguin, 1975.

Bakeless, Katherine and John, *Spies of the Revolution*: New York: Scholastic, 1962.

Bucher, Lloyd, *My Story*: New York: Doubleday, 1970.

Collins, Larry, and Lapierre, Dominique, *Is Paris Burning?* New York: Simon & Schuster, 1965.

Dulles, Allen, *The Craft of Intelligence*: New York: Harper & Row, 1963.

Dulles, Allen, *Great True Spy Stories*: London, Robson Books, 1984.

Gramont, Sanche de, *The Secret War*: New York: Putnam's, 1962.

Kneece, Jack, *The Walker Spy Case*: New York: Stein & Day, 1986.

Le Carré, John, *The Spy Who Came in from the Cold*: New York: Coward-McCann, 1964.

Lindsey, Robert, *The Falcon and the Snowman*: New York: Simon & Schuster, 1979.

Meeropol, Robert and Michael, *We Are Your Sons*: Boston, Houghton Mifflin, 1975.

Nizer, Louis, *The Implosion Conspiracy*: New York: Doubleday, 1973.

Philby, Kim, *My Silent War*: New York: Grove Press, 1968.

Schneir, Walter and Miriam, *Invitation to an Inquest*: New York: Doubleday, 1965.

Stevenson, William, *A Man Called Intrepid: The Secret War 1939–1945*. New York: Harcourt Brace Jovanovich, 1976.

Uris, Leon, *Topaz*: New York: Bantam, 1981.

INDEX

Abakumov, Gen. V. S., 41
Abel, Rudolf, 14, 21–22, 84, 85, 92–96
Acheson, Dean, 29
Allende, Salvador, 17
American Revolution, 12, 27–28, 85
Andropov, Yuri, 38
Angleton, James Jesus, 76
Arens, Moshe, 127
Armey, Dick, 113
Arnold, Benedict, 12, 28
Assassinations, 16, 38, 109
Atomic Energy Act of 1946, 54
Atom spies, 44–52, 58
Azpillaga, Florentino, 74

Baker, Lafayette, 28
Bancroft, Edward, 27–28
Barbie, Klaus, 15–16
Bay of Pigs invasion, 17, 67
Becker, Howard, 58
Bentley, Elizabeth, 46, 47, 48, 50
Beria, Lavrenti, 38, 73
Berlin Tunnel, 60–61
Black Chamber, 29
Blake, George, 60–62
Bloch, Emanuel, 53, 54
Blunt, Anthony, 22, 75, 79
Boone, James, 11
Bourke, Sean, 61
Boyce, Christopher, 101, 102, 103, 104–7, 114, 128
Bozart, Jim, 93–94
Brooke, Gerald, 67
Bucher, Lloyd M., 68, 70–71
"Bugs," 108–13
Burgess, Guy, 22, 73, 76, 79–80, 83

Carter, Jimmy, 36
Carver, George, 23
Casey, William, 18, 19
Castro, Fidel, 17, 109
Central Intelligence Agency (CIA), 12, 16–19, 23–24, 29–32, 34–35, 62, 67–68, 75–76, 80, 99–100, 108, 127–29
Chafee, John H., 71
Chambers, Whittaker, 45, 46, 48
Chebrikov, Viktor, 42
Chile, 16–17
Chin, Larry Wu-tai, 124–25
Civil War, 28
Colby, William, 34, 76
Communications equipment, 113
Computer bugging, 111
Copeland, Miles, 109
Coplon, Judith, 46
Counter-intelligence, 16
Covert operations, 16–19, 34–35
Cover-ups, 23
Cuba, 17, 64, 67
Cumming, Sir Mansfield, 15

Daniloff, Nicholas, 36, 42, 86, 87
Day-Lewis, Cecil, 79
Defectors, 20, 41–42, 45–46, 60, 72–83
Diem, Ngo Dinh, 16
Dirty tricks, 23–24, 109
Dolnytsin, Anatoli, 60
Dominican Republic, 16
Donovan, James B., 85, 95–96
Donovan, Col. William J., 30
Double agents, 27–28, 60–62, 64, 66, 72–73, 76–83
Douglas, William O., 54

141

"Drops," 21, 27, 93
Dulles, Allen, 17, 67, 85

Eban, Abba, 125
Eisenhower, Dwight D., 35, 54, 90, 92
Eitan, Rafael, 126, 127
Elitcher, Max, 51
Espionage Act of 1917, 29, 54
Executions of spies, 26–27
Exposure of spies, 20–21, 45–46, 60–64, 66–67
Expulsions of spies, 86–88

Falcon and Snowman case, 100–7
Ferguson, Thomas, 101
Fiers, Alan D., 18–19
Fleming, Ian, 11, 39
Foxman, Abraham H., 125
France, 15
Franklin, Benjamin, 27
Frolik, Josef, 74
Fuchs, Klaus, 22, 48, 49, 50
Future of espionage, 129–30

Gee, Elizabeth, 63, 64
Gehlen Organization, 15, 16, 60
George, Claire, 18
Germany, 12, 15–16, 60
Gold, Harry, 49, 50, 51, 53, 56–57
Golitsyn, Anatoliy, 75–76
Gouzenko, Igor, 45–46, 48
Great Britain, 12, 15, 46, 50, 60–64, 66–67, 76–83
Greenglass, David, 49, 50–51, 52, 57
Greenglass, Ruth, 51–52
Grishin, Boris, 105
Guatemala, 16

Hale, Nathan, 12, 85
Harris, Stephen, 71
Hasenfus, Eugene, 35
Hayhanen, Reino, 14, 21, 93, 94
Helms, Richard, 100
Hiss, Alger, 45, 46, 48

History of espionage, 11–12
Hodges, Duane D., 68
Hoover, J. Edgar, 82
Houghton, Harry, 62–63, 64
House Un-American Activities Committee, 47, 48, 58
Howard, Edward Lee, 124
Hunt, E. Howard, 17
Hydrophones, 115–16

Iran, 16
Iran Contra scandal, 17–19, 23
Israel, 15, 125–27

Jenner, William, 48
Joannides, George, 98
Johnson, C. L., 88

Kampiles, William, 98–99, 107, 114
Kaufman, Irving, 52, 53
Kennan, George F., 108
Kennedy, John, 17, 64, 67, 96
KGB (Soviet state security), 12, 25–27, 32, 36–37, 38–43, 60, 73–74
KH-11 satellite system, 98–100, 107, 114
Khrushchev, Nikita S., 38, 64, 90, 92
Korea, North, 68–71
Koski, Walter, 57
Kravshenko, Victor, 44
Kroger, Helen and Peter, 22, 63, 67

Laser beam bugging, 111
Lebonitte, Vincent, 58
Lee, Andrew Daulton, 101–2, 104–6, 114
Lincoln, Abraham, 28
Lindsey, Robert, 101, 115
Linschitz, Henry, 57
Lonetree, Clayton, 25, 26, 27
Lonsdale, Gordon, 22, 62, 63, 66
Ludwig, Kurt F., 21
Lumumba, Patrice, 16

McCarthy, Joseph, 47–48

Index

McCone, John A., 17, 67
McCord, James, 17
Maclean, Donald, 22, 73, 76, 79, 80, 83
McNamara, Robert, 70
Marcus, Miron, 68
Marine Sex for Secrets case, 25–27
Martin, William H., 72
Mata Hari, 12
May, Alan Nunn, 46
Meeropol, Robert and Michael, 56
Microchips, 116–17
Microdots, 93, 114
Microphones, directional, 110
Microwave bugging, 110, 111
Miller, Richard, 13, 124, 129
Mitchell, George J., 19
Mitchell, Vernon F., 72
Morrison, Philip, 57
Moscow Embassy, U.S., 25–26, 112, 113
Myths about espionage, 12–15, 20, 24

Nasser, Gamal Abdel, 109
National Detective Police, 28
National Security Act of 1947, 31, 34
National Security Agency, 72
National Security Council (NSC), 17, 31, 35
Nazi spies, 15–16, 20–21
Nicaragua, 17
Nixon, Richard M., 105
Nizer, Louis, 56
Norman, Alan Van, 68
North, Lt. Col. Oliver, 18, 19
Nosenko, Yuri, 75, 76

Office of Strategic Services (OSS), 15, 30, 44
Ogorodnikova, Svetlana, 13, 14, 124
Orlov, Alexander, 73

Pearl Harbor, attack on, 29–30
Pelton, Ronald, 34, 124, 129
Penkovsky, Oleg, 64, 65, 66
Peres, Shimon, 127

Petrov, Vladimir, 73–74
Philby, Eleanor, 77–78, 81, 82
Philby, Kim, 22, 73, 75, 76–83
Pinkerton, Allan, 28
Planes for spying, 88–89, 115
Plausible deniability, 35, 90
Poindexter, Adm. John, 18, 19
Poland, 62
Pollard, Jonathan J., 22, 125, 126
Pollard spy case, 22, 125–27
Pontecorvo, Bruno, 58
Portland naval secrets case, 62–64, 66–67
Powers, Gary Francis, 35, 84, 85, 88, 89–90, 91, 92
Prosecution of spies, 33, 51–52, 122
Pryor, Frederic, 96
Pueblo incident, 68–71
Pyramider Project, 104

Rabin, Yitzhak, 127
Reagan, Ronald, 17, 19, 86, 113
Rhyolite satellite, 115
Rickover, Adm. Hyman G., 32–33
Roosevelt, Franklin D., 30, 46, 48
Rosenberg, Ethel and Julius, 49, 51–59
Rosenberg Law, 33, 58
Rosenberg spy ring, 48–52
Roth, William, 129
Russell, Richard, 70

Sanni, Violetta, 25
Satellites for spying, 98–100, 107, 114–15
Schlesinger, James R., 34, 113
Schneir, Miriam and Walter, 56
"Screech," 113
Secure rooms, 110
Sella, Col. Aviem, 126–27
Senate Internal Security Subcommittee, 48
Shamir, Yitzhak, 125, 127
Ships for spying, 68
Shultz, George, 19
Signals intelligence, 114–15
Smith, Gen. Walter Bedell, 24, 80, 83

143

"Sneaky," 108
Sobell, Morton, 51, 52
Soble, Jack and Myra, 58
Sorge, Richard, 12
Soviet intelligence services, 37–38.
  See also KGB
Soviet spies in the U.S., 44–48
Spears, George, 97
Spies who don't know they are spies, 31–32
Spy gadgets, 13, 20, 63, 98–100, 108–16
SR-71 spy plane, 115
Stalin, Joseph, 12, 30, 38, 73
Stimson, Henry L., 29
Stockell, James B., 129
Submarines, 68, 115–16
Sullivan, Kaye and Jerry, 106–7
Swaps of captured spies, 61, 64, 66–67, 84–86, 87, 90, 92, 95–97

Tallmadge, Maj. Benjamin, 28
Technology thefts, 39, 116–17
Teller, Edward, 57
Thompson, Robert Glen, 67–68
Tkachenko, Aleksey, 118, 119–20
Tompkins, William F., 85
Toth, Robert, 36, 37
Townsend, Robert, 28
Traitor-spies, 22–23, 25–27, 31–32, 48–52, 53–59, 62–67, 76–83, 100–107, 118–24, 129
Trotsky, Leon, 38

Trujillo, Gen. Rafael, 16
Truman, Harry S., 30–31
TRW, 101, 102, 104, 128
Turner, Stansfield, 100

U.S. intelligence services, 27–29.
  See also Central Intelligence Agency
U-2 spy case, 84–85, 88–92, 96–97

Vassall, William John, 60, 75
Vietnam war, 16
Von Raab, William, 116

Walker spy ring, 22, 39, 118–24
Walsingham, Sir Francis, 12
Washington, George, 28
Watergate scandal, 17, 105–6
Wennerstrom Stig, 67
White, Harry Dexter, 46
Whitworth, Jerry, 119, 120, 122, 123 129
Wolfson, Nikolai, 124
World War I, 12
World War II, 12, 29–30, 44–45, 48–49
Wynne, Greville, 64, 66

Yakovlev, Anatoli, 49, 52, 56
Yurchenko, Vitali, 123

Zaire, 16
Zakharov, Gennadi, 86, 87

UF
1525
.I6
S55
1988

#1290